W9-DEW-891

FRENCH BISTRO COOKING

JOHN VARNOM

FRENCH BISTRO COOKING

JOHN VARNOM

CHARTWELL
BOOKS, INC.

For Richard, Mick, Adam, Pete, Ken,
Bob, Giorgio, Jackie, Neller and Gerald.
With very special thanks to Deidre
Slevin and Helga Roehrs.

A QUINTET BOOK

Published by Chartwell Books
A Division of Book Sales, Inc.
110 Enterprise Avenue
Secaucus, New Jersey 07094

Copyright © 1988 Quintet Publishing Limited.
All rights reserved. No part of this publication
may be reproduced, stored in a retrieval system
or transmitted in any form or by any means,
electronic, mechanical, photocopying, recording
or otherwise, without the permission of the
copyright holder.

ISBN 1-55521-325-1

This book was designed and produced by
Quintet Publishing Limited
6 Blundell Street
London N7 9BH

Design Director: Peter Bridgewater
Art Director: Ian Hunt
Designer: Helen White
Editors: Caroline Beattie, Judith Simons,
Susie Ward
Photographer: Trevor Wood
Food Preparation and Styling: Jonathan Higgins,
Judith Kelsey

Typeset in Great Britain by
Central Southern Typesetters, Eastbourne
Manufactured in Hong Kong by
Regent Publishing Services Limited
Printed in Hong Kong by
South Sea International Press Ltd

Contents

Introduction

Since the title of this book is 'French Bistro Cooking', it seems reasonable to begin it by asking what a French bistro is. A simple question, you might think. But a simple question is a little like the Indian Ocean on a tranquil afternoon: a placid and agreeable surface beneath which a surly and intractable crowd of rapacious fish is hanging about with its collective mouth open.

Perhaps we should start with the etymology and a little history. The bistro, it seems, first became popular in 1940s Paris, when it might have been a café, or a snack bar, or even a small restaurant. It is worth pointing out here that café, in French, does not indicate an establishment that serves food. Drinks are all you can guarantee at cafés.

Etymologically, there are a couple of possibilities in French. There is a word bastringue, which means a small dance hall. Unlikely, in my view. There is bistre, which rather disappointingly turns out to be a surgical instrument. There is a verb bistouiller, which means to make up concoctions. It also carries the sense that these concoctions are at least laughable and usually unpleasant.

No, the likeliest contender seems not to be French at all, but Russian. Bistro is Russian for 'quick'. And dimly reported to us through the mists of antiquity is the fact that Russian troops, entering Paris in 1815 or thereabouts, were all yelling 'bistro' at the top of their voices. They were starving, and they wanted sustenance in a hurry.

Can it be, then, that a bistro is a place you can get quick French food? This is another simple question.

Some dishes can undoubtedly be prepared quickly. Moules marinières, for example, grilled steak, pommes allumettes. But I think we might all agree that a plate of escargots would be another piece of typical bistro fare. And it is certainly true that, once prepared, they can be baked and served within no more than ten minutes of being ordered.

The catch here is 'once prepared'. As the recipe for Escargots Bourguignonnes shows, snails take several hours, if not days, to organize from scratch. Our bistro chef has simply done what every other good cook should: prepare carefully beforehand to make service as quick as possible. In and out of restaurants, this is a golden rule.

So simple speed does not a bistro make. Nor does the absence of serious preparation for service, which in any event is almost impossible if you're using fresh ingredients. What then?

Simplicity? Perhaps bistro food is somehow simpler than other restaurants. But simpler how? Hollandaise is a simple sauce when you consider its basic ingredients: egg yolks and butter. But amateur cooks seem to think it is difficult. Why? Because, I suppose that if it goes wrong, which it can easily do, there's nothing much you can do about it. So 'simple' here seems to mean something you don't have to do carefully. That idea we can throw out immediately: all cooking should be careful, bistro or not.

In terms of the actual food and cooking, there are two other areas to consider. The first is economy in the kitchen, good housekeeping. The use, for example, of meat scraps for soups or terrines, of vegetable trimmings for stocks and so forth. But as with preparation, this should be common practice for cooks everywhere. To discard perfectly usable by-products is not high-falutin', it is just profligate.

Indeed, good housekeeping may even be a mark of the more, and not the less, expensive restaurant these days. Cheaper restaurants will almost certainly be more inclined to buy pre-packed, pre-cut steaks and muddle through with stock cubes, whereas the more expensive will do things as they should be done – will bone, will butcher and get much better margins into the bargain.

Which finally leads us to the remaining point, expense, and maybe a definition. We have seen that bistros are neither quicker nor slower than the other places, whomsoever they may be. The preparation depends on the skill and professionalism of the chef and the integrity of the management, as does the housekeeping. It's just that the bistro should be cheaper, we feel, and the menu less cushioned with foie gras or studded with truffles. But how can we tell as we stand outside?

It's easy. Bistros are just restaurants without tablecloths.

Soups

Onion Soup Gratinée 9

Thick Carrot Soup Crécy Style 10

Thick White Bean Soup Soissons Style 11

Asparagus Soup 12

Creamed Watercress Soup 13

Sorrel or Spinach Soup 13

Leek and Potato Soup 14

Creamed Mushroom Soup 15

Shrimp Bisque 16

Provençal Fish Soup 17

Onion Soup Gratinée

SOUPE À L'OIGNON GRATINÉE

SERVES 6

Cooking time 20 minutes

INGREDIENTS

½ cup/100 g/¼ lb butter

2 cloves garlic, crushed

900 g/2 lb onions

75 ml/5 tbsp flour

6 slices crustless bread, preferably white and French

⅔ cup/75 g/3 oz grated Gruyère cheese

Salt and pepper to taste

PREPARATION

▪ Melt the butter over a medium heat. Add the garlic and onions and fry until golden brown; add the flour and fry it until golden.

▪ Add 10 cups/2.25 L/4 pt of hot water. Season with salt and pepper and cook at a rolling boil until the onions are tender. Skim off any fat.

▪ Place a slice of bread in the bottom of each of 6 soup bowls and sprinkle over the grated cheese. Pour on the soup – make sure that it is boiling freely – and allow to stand for 5–6 minutes.

COOK'S TIPS

This simple but excellent soup can be 'improved' in all sorts of ways. You can add sherry or brandy or use stock instead of water. But with good, strongly flavoured onions, there is no real need. One thing you can do, however, is to put the bread and cheese on top of the soup and pop the bowls into a very hot oven or under the grill (broiler). Just make sure they're fireproof. They'll be very hot, too, so warn your guests and watch your fingers.

Thick Carrot Soup Crécy Style

SOUPE CRECY

SERVES 6
Cooking time 1½ hours
INGREDIENTS
100 g/¼ lb lean unsmoked bacon
1 medium onion
1 kg/2¼ lb carrots
10 cups/2.25 L/4 pt stock (*see* Stocks and Glazes)
½ cup/120 ml/4 fl oz double (heavy) cream
Salt and pepper to taste

PREPARATION

▪ Dice the bacon and the onion and sweat both together over a low heat for about 10 minutes. As the bacon and onions are cooking slice the carrots finely.

▪ Add the carrots to the mixture, cover and cook for a further 10 minutes at the same low heat.

▪ Add the stock, cover and simmer slowly for 1 hour.

▪ Press the mixture through a fine sieve (strainer) or liquidize, then return to the heat. Whisk in the cream, season and serve immediately.

CHEF'S ASIDE

Anything *de Crécy* denotes the presence of carrots, for Crécy is a northern French town famous for its carrots. This is a mark of distinction in an area of mixed rural economy, not unlike a small stretch of sea being famous for its water.

Thick White Bean Soup Soissons Style

POTAGE SOISSONAIS

SERVES 8

Cooking time 1½–2 hours

Pre-preparation time 2 hours

INGREDIENTS

350 g/¾ lb dried white beans

1 onion, roughly chopped

1 carrot, roughly chopped

6¼ cups/1.4 L/2½ pt stock
(*see* Stocks and Glazes)

1¼ cups/300 ml/½ pt milk

¼ cup/60 ml/2 fl oz double
(heavy) cream

60 ml/4 tbsp tomato purée
(paste)

60 ml/4 tbsp butter

Salt and pepper to taste

PREPARATION

▊ *Wash the beans thoroughly and leave to soak for 2 hours. After soaking, cover with water.*
▊ *Add the carrot and onion and cook until soft – about 1½ hours. Press the mixture through a fine sieve (strainer) or liquidize.*
▊ *Add the milk and the stock. Return to the heat. When the soup boils, whisk in the cream and the tomato purée (paste).*
▊ *Off the heat, whisk in the butter, check the seasoning and serve immediately.*

COOK'S TIPS

As you read on through the soup recipes, you will see that some call for the addition of cream or butter at the last moment. If you are not serving the soup immediately, do not add these ingredients. They are strictly last-minute items. Reason? Over time the cream may curdle and you'll lose the soup. Butter will split if the soup is re-boiled.

Asparagus Soup
CREME D'ASPERGES

SERVES 6

Cooking time 1 hour

INGREDIENTS

60 ml/4 tbsp butter

90 ml/6 tbsp plain (all-purpose) flour

1.4 L/2½ pt light stock (*see* Stocks and Glazes)

450 g/1 lb asparagus

⅔ cup/150 ml/¼ pt double (heavy) cream

Salt and pepper to taste

PREPARATION

▌ *Make a light roux with the butter and flour (see Roux). Slowly add the stock and bring the mixture to the boil. Turn down the heat.*
▌ *Cut the heads from the asparagus and set aside. Cut away the tough, whitish bottoms and discard. Chop the remaining green parts and add to the roux and stock.*
▌ *Simmer the mixture for about 50 minutes, then liquidize or force through a sieve (strainer). Return the mixture to a low heat.*
▌ *Blanch the asparagus heads in boiling, salted water for about 5 minutes.*
▌ *Before serving, stir the cream into the soup and season with the salt and pepper. Serve very hot, garnished with the asparagus heads.*

Creamed Watercress Soup

SOUPE CRESSONIERE

SERVES 6
Cooking time 1 hour
INGREDIENTS
60 ml/4 tbsp butter
100 g/¼ lb onions
White part of 1 medium leek
900 g/2 lb potatoes
10 cups/2.25 L/4 pt stock (*see* Stocks and Glazes)
4 bunches watercress, well washed
⅔ cup/150 ml/¼ pt double (heavy) cream
Salt and pepper to taste

PREPARATION

▪ *Melt the butter over a low heat. Shred the onions and the leek finely and sweat in the butter without browning them.*

▪ *Peel and slice the potatoes. Add to the leek mixture, then add the stock. Bring the mixture to the boil and skim if necessary.*

▪ *Add the watercress and boil rapidly so the potatoes break down. When they no longer hold their shape, press the mixture through a fine sieve (strainer) or liquidize it.*

▪ *Replace on the heat, whisk in the cream and season. Serve immediately.*

Sorrel or Spinach Soup

SOUPE A L'OSEILLE OU AUX EPINARDS

SERVES 6
Cooking time 1 hour
INGREDIENTS
60 ml/4 tbsp butter
White part of 1 leek
675 g/1½ lb potatoes
9 cups/2 L/3½ pt stock (*see* Stocks and Glazes)
225 g/½ lb fresh sorrel or spinach – which can be frozen
½ cup/120 ml/4 fl oz double (heavy) cream
Salt and pepper to taste

PREPARATION

▪ *Melt the butter over a low heat. Slice the leek and potatoes and sweat them in the butter for 10 minutes. Add the stock and cook slowly until soft.*

▪ *Chop the sorrel or the spinach finely. Stew it slowly in its own juices in a separate pan. Use no butter but stir occasionally to prevent any tendency to stick or singe.*

▪ *After 10 minutes' cooking add the stewed vegetables. Skim if necessary, season, whisk in the cream and serve immediately.*

Leek and Potato Soup

POTAGE PARMENTIER

SERVES 6

Cooking time 1 hour

INGREDIENTS

½ cup/100 g/¼ lb butter

3 medium leeks, washed and sliced

1 kg/2¼ lb potatoes, skinned and sliced

6¼ cups/1.4 L/2½ pt stock (*see* Stocks and Glazes)

½ cup/120 ml/4 fl oz double or single (heavy or light) cream

Salt and pepper to taste

2 slices of the crustless bread of your choice

PREPARATION

■ Melt half the butter over a high heat until foaming. Brown the leeks well in the butter. Add the potatoes to the leeks and butter. Sprinkle with salt and pepper, add the stock and simmer the soup slowly without covering, until the potatoes are very soft.

■ Press the soup through a fine sieve (strainer) or liquidize. Return to a low heat. If it is too thick, dilute it a little with water.

■ Heat the remaining butter in a frying pan (skillet). Cut the bread into dice and fry until golden. Set aside.

■ Whisk the cream into the soup and season. Serve immediately with the fried bread (croûtons) as a garnish.

Creamed Mushroom Soup

CRÈME CAPUCINE OU CRÈME AUX CHAMPIGNONS

SERVES 6

Cooking time 45 minutes

INGREDIENTS

90 ml/5 tbsp butter

½ cup/65 g/2½ oz plain (all-purpose) flour

6¼ cups/1.4 L/2½ pt stock (*see* Stocks and Glazes)

Juice of 1 lemon

350 g/¾ lb fresh mushrooms

⅔ cup/150 ml/¼ pt double (heavy) cream

Salt and pepper to taste

PREPARATION

▉ *Make a velouté with 60 ml/4 tbsp of the butter, the flour and the stock (see Béchamels and Veloutés).*
▉ *Combine the lemon juice and the remaining butter in a frying pan (skillet) large enough to hold the mushrooms at a low heat.*
▉ *Wash and finely chop the mushrooms and then cook them in the butter and lemon until all the liquid has evaporated – the mushrooms will contribute some of their own.*
▉ *Add the cooked mushrooms to the velouté and cook at a gentle simmer for a further 15 minutes. Whisk in the cream, season and serve immediately.*

CHEF'S ASIDE

Why is Crème aux Champignons also called Crème Capucine? Some say that the colour of the soup resembles the pale, creamy brown of the Capucin monk's habit. But this explanation is hard to sustain, as a clear consommé of chicken garnished with strips of lettuce and spinach is also known as Consommé Capucine. 'Capucine', as well as denoting a nun of the Capucin order, is actually French for 'nasturtium', a flower whose peppery leaves often do feature in salads.

Shrimp Bisque
BISQUE DE CREVETTES

SERVES 6

Cooking time 2 hours

INGREDIENTS

450 g/1 lb prawn or shrimp shells (*see* Brochette of Prawns)

90 ml/5 tbsp butter

1 small carrot

1 medium onion

1 bay leaf

60 ml/4 tbsp chopped parsley

60 ml/2 fl oz brandy

Good ½ cup/50 g/2 oz plain (all-purpose) flour

90 ml/5 tbsp tomato purée (paste)

⅔ cup/150 ml/¼ pt double (heavy) cream

PREPARATION

▮ *Boil the prawn or shrimp shells for 1 hour in 6¼ cups 1.4 L/2½ pt unsalted water.*

▮ *In the meantime, melt the butter in a 4½ cup/2 L/3 pt saucepan over a low heat. Add the carrot and the onion, very finely chopped, the bay leaf and the parsley, and stew very gently for about 10 minutes. Add the brandy and remove from the heat.*

▮ *After 1 hour, strain the prawn shells and top up the broth with water up to a quantity of 5 cups/1.15 L/2 pt.*

▮ *Add the flour to the butter, vegetables and brandy mixture and cook gently for 3–4 minutes. Slowly add the shell broth and bring the liquid to the boil.*

▮ *Add the tomato purée (paste), then liquidize the mixture or force through a fine sieve (strainer). Return the mixture to the heat, whisk in the cream and serve immediately.*

COOK'S TIPS

The soup should need no salt. And if you have saved a few whole, shelled shrimp or prawns for a garnish, so much the better.
You might find it a bore to save shrimp shells. So why not make the broth when you eat the shrimp and reduce it by boiling to a manageable size? Then freeze it.

Provençal Fish Soup

SOUPE DE POISSON PROVENÇALE

SERVES 6
Cooking time 1 hour
INGREDIENTS
450 g/1 lb white fish trimmings
1 large onion
30 ml/2 tbsp chopped parsley
2 bay leaves
Juice of 1 lemon
10 white peppercorns
¾ cup/175 g/6 oz tomato purée (paste)
30 ml/2 tbsp paprika
1 pinch saffron or turmeric
Salt and pepper to taste

PREPARATION

▮ Put the fish, the onion, peeled and halved, the parsley, bay leaves, lemon juice and white wine into 5 Am pt/ 2.25 L/4 pt water and bring to the boil. Turn down the heat and simmer gently for 25–30 minutes.

▮ Add the peppercorns and let the broth stand for 5 minutes or so. Strain, discard all the debris and replace the broth on high heat.

▮ Add the tomato purée or paste, paprika and saffron or turmeric. Reduce the broth by one-third. Season to taste with salt and pepper. This soup can be made ahead and reheated – this also gives the flavours time to combine and mature.

COOK'S TIPS

This soup is traditionally served with three accompaniments which, as accompaniments go, are among the most inspired in the French kitchen. They are: *Rouille*, a mayonnaise strongly flavoured with cayenne pepper and garlic and coloured with paprika (*see* Mayonnaise). Toasted French bread. Grated Gruyère cheese. You are not getting a recipe for these latter two items. But you are getting a ·wine recommendation: chilled rosé, preferably from Provence.

Cold and Warm Appetizers

Salade Nicoise 19

Cold Vegetables in White Wine, Olive Oil,
Lemon and Parsley 20

Salmon Mousse Chaud-Froid 21

Terrine of Pork Livers and Brandy 22

Chicken Livers in Aspic 24

Warm Salad of Duck & Chicken Mignons 24

Warm Salad of Sweetcorn and
Chicken Livers 25

Snails in their Shells with Garlic and Parsley
Butter 26

Snails in Puff Pastry 27

Poached Sweetbreads in an Onion Case 28

Mussels in White Wine, Parsley and Shallots 30

Frogs' Legs Sautéed with Parsley, Butter and
Lemon 31

Leek Tart 31

Salade Niçoise

SERVES 6

Preparation time about
30 minutes

INGREDIENTS

450 g/1 lb potatoes

450 g/1 lb string beans

4 medium tomatoes

6 anchovy fillets

12 green, pitted olives

3 hard-boiled eggs

1¼ cups/300 ml/½ pt
vinaigrette (*see* Vinaigrette)

PREPARATION

▋ *Cook the potatoes in their skins in salted water. Remove when still firm, peel and cut into small dice.*
▋ *Cut the beans into squares, cook in salted water until soft, cool and drain.*
▋ *Mix the vegetables, dress with the vinaigrette and heap together in a salad bowl.*
▋ *Decorate with the tomatoes cut into quarters, the anchovy fillets, halved olives and the eggs, also cut into quarters.*
▋ OPTIONAL EXTRAS *Chunks of tuna, grilled (broiled) fresh, preserved in oil, or canned, can also be added to this dish. And the best wine would be a chilled rosé, preferably from Provence (where the best French rosé comes from).*

COOK'S TIPS

The potatoes should still
be warm when you dress
them with the
vinaigrette, which they
will then absorb more
freely.

Cold Vegetables in White Wine, Olive Oil, Lemon and Parsley

LEGUMES A LA GRECQUE

SERVES 2—22

Cooking time 20 minutes
minimum

INGREDIENTS

²⁄₃ cup/150 ml/¼ pt white
wine

⅓ cup/50 ml/2 fl oz olive oil

1 sprig parsley, finely chopped

²⁄₃ cup/150 ml/¼ pt water

Juice of 1 lemon

1 bay leaf

6 black peppercorns

Salt to taste

Selection of fresh vegetables

PREPARATION

▧ *Blanch your choice of vegetables and dress them in the marinade (see Cook's Tips).*

BLANCHING TABLE		
Asparagus	tips only	8 minutes
Aubergines (eggplants)	do not use	
Broccoli	florets (flowerets)	2 minutes
Carrots	batons	3 minutes
Cauliflower	florets (flowerets)	4 minutes
Courgettes (zucchini)	batons	do not blanch
Fennel	diced	6 minutes
French (green) beans	whole	5 minutes
Mange-tout (snow peas)	whole	1 minute
Mushrooms	sliced	do not blanch
Onions	sliced	4 minutes
Peppers	sliced	4 minutes
Root vegetables	small dice	4 minutes

COOK'S TIPS

All vegetables suit this dish, except anything from the cabbage family or highly-dyed vegetables such as beetroot, whose colours will run. The following table shows the cuts and blanching times for the selection you will be most likely to use – or find, if it comes to that. Blanch in boiling, salted water.

Salmon Mousse Chaud-Froid

MOUSSE DE SAUMON EN CHAUD-FROID

SERVES 4
Cooking time 12–15 minutes
Setting time about 1 hour
INGREDIENTS
350 g/¾ lb skinned and boned fresh salmon
1¼ cups/300 ml/½ pt double (heavy) cream
12 sprigs of fresh dill or basil
Salt and coarsely ground black pepper
Cayenne pepper
1¼ cups/300 ml/½ pt fish velouté (see Béchamels and Veloutés)
or
1¼ cups/300 ml/½ pt Béchamel (see Béchamels and Veloutés)
⅔ cup/150 ml/¼ pt stiff aspic jelly (gelatin) (see Aspics and Chaud-Froids)
60 ml/4 tbsp butter

PREPARATION

▨ *Mash the salmon meat as finely as you can. (Use a blender or food processor, if available.) It should be entirely paste-like. Whip the cream and fold it into the salmon.*

▨ *Finely chop half the basil or dill, add to the mixture and season highly with the salt, black pepper and the cayenne. Taste it for yourself to assess seasoning; the mixture is perfectly edible even raw.*

▨ *Line 4 ramekins with the melted butter and force the fish mixture well down into each one.*

▨ *Set the ramekins in a frying pan (skillet) on top of the stove, fill the pan with boiling water to within 1 cm/½ in of the top of the ramekins and cover the whole pan well.*

▨ *Poach very gently – the water must not bubble over into the fish – for 12-15 minutes. It will be cooked when the mixture shrinks away from the sides of the pot.*

▨ *Remove the mousses from the ramekins and set aside to chill.*

TO COAT WITH THE CHAUD-FROID SAUCE

▨ *Heat the velouté or béchamel to just under boiling and stir in the aspic jelly (gelatin). Season highly with salt, pepper and cayenne and allow to cool until lukewarm.*

▨ *Using a pastry brush, paint the chilled mousses with the sauce in a series of thin layers. (If the mousses are sufficiently chilled and the layers sufficiently thin, the sauce will set practically on contact.) Coat until the fish is completely masked.*

▨ *Your final gesture: a brush-stroke on top of each mousse, into which you set a basil leaf or sprig of dill.*

ONE COOK'S TIP AND ONE LAW OF NATURE

If your chaud-froid won't set and your quantities were right, then the mousse wasn't cold enough, or the chaud-froid wasn't lukewarm, or the layers were too thick, or all three.
Secondly, the law: all we did was liquidize, season and poach, a universal principle applicable to all fish and white meat too.
Just remember to season highly to avoid blandness. All seasoning loses its strength (as transmitted through the tastebuds) when it is chilled. Under-seasoning therefore results in undesirable blandness – or subtlety, as the emperor's-new-clothes school of restaurant critics call it.

Terrine of Pork Livers and Brandy

TERRINE DE FOIE DE PORC

Cooking time about 1¼ hours

Oven temperature 175° C/
350° F/Gas 4

INGREDIENTS

225 g/½ lb pig's liver

100 g/¼ lb unsmoked bacon

2 cups/100 g/4 oz crustless
white bread, torn into small
pieces

⅔ cup/150 ml/¼ pt milk

1 large onion

2 eggs

1 teaspoon each chopped
parsley, dried thyme and dried
marjoram

⅓ cup/60 ml/2 fl oz brandy

PREPARATION

■ Preheat the oven. Grind or process the liver and the bacon together finely.
■ Soak the bread in milk and squeeze dry and at the same time boil the onion in salted water until soft. Grind or process the bread and onion together and combine with the ground meats.
■ Place the whole mixture in a mixing bowl, beat in two eggs and blend in the herbs and the brandy.
■ Put the mixture in a baking dish just large enough to hold it. Place the filled dish in a second dish of about double the capacity but with sides of a similar height. Fill the second dish with boiling water to within ½ in/1 cm of the top of the smaller dish.
■ Cover both dishes securely with either lids or baking foil and cook in a pre-heated oven. For a denser texture, let the terrine stand for 10 minutes after cooking. Then press firmly down over the whole surface area for 30 seconds or so.
■ Set the terrine aside in a cool place. Turn it out when cold and wrap in cling film (plastic wrap) if not serving immediately.

COOK'S TIPS

There seems to be something about pâtés and terrines which terrifies people. Don't let them. They are simply a splendid way of getting rid of trimmings. There are only three things to remember and one taboo to overcome.

■ Terrines are just a mixture of things ground up together and then bound, usually with egg.
■ Since they are served cold, they should be more highly seasoned than their hot counterparts (see Salmon Mousse Cook's Tip).
■ They are always cooked slowly in bains-marie. And if there's no space in the oven, you can do them on top of the stove.

Finally, the taboo. Once you start to experiment with other mixtures, you will have to check your own seasoning. This means tasting the mixture raw.

Chicken Livers in Aspic
LES FOIES DE VOLAILLE EN GELEE

SERVES .6

Cooking time 2–3 hours

INGREDIENTS

60 ml/4 tbsp butter

2 cloves fresh garlic, crushed

2 sprigs of parsley, chopped finely

1 small onion, chopped finely

6 chicken livers

⅔ cup/150 ml/¼ pt white wine

2 cups/450 ml/¾ pt light stock (see Stocks and Glazes)

or

stock (bouillon) cube dissolved in 2 cups/450 ml/ ¾ pt water

8 leaves gelatine

PREPARATION

▪ Melt the butter in a frying pan (skillet) at a low heat. Add garlic and parsley; stew gently for a minute or so.
▪ Turn up the heat to full and toss in the chopped onion. As soon as the onions begin to sizzle, add the chicken livers and seal them on both sides.
▪ Turn the heat back to a medium flame and sauté the livers for 3 minutes on either side. Pour off any fat from the pan. Place the livers, onions, parsley and garlic on a plate.
▪ Make an aspic solution with the gelatin(e), white wine and stock (see Aspics and Chaud-Froids).
▪ Place the chicken livers side by side lengthways along the bottom of a terrine dish. Alternatively, place each liver in an individual ramekin about twice the volume of the liver.
▪ Sprinkle equal amounts of the garlic, parsley and onion over each liver. Pour over the aspic solution until the livers are completely covered. Chill the dish or the ramekins for 2 to 3 hours or until set.

COOK'S TIP

Aspics can be freed by warming the container until the first film of aspic melts. Dip them quickly in hot water.

Warm Salad of Duck and Chicken Mignons
SALADE TIEDE DES MIGNONS DE VOLAILLE ET DE CANARD

SERVES 4

Cooking time 5 minutes

INGREDIENTS

75 ml/4½ tbsp walnut oil

30 ml/2 tbsp butter

8 duck mignons (see Boning)

8 chicken mignons (see Boning)

60 ml/4 tbsp green peppercorns

1 frisée lettuce

1 head of radicchio (argula)

2 medium heads of chicory (Belgian endive)

75 ml/4½ tbsp vinaigrette (see Vinaigrette)

Salt and pepper to taste

PREPARATION

▪ Amalgamate the oil and butter in a frying pan (skillet) over a high heat. Toss in the mignons, sauté for 2½ minutes per side, and add the green peppercorns. Remove the pan from the heat.
▪ Arrange the frisée and radicchio (argula) in heaps in the middle of each plate with the leaves of chicory (Belgian endive) fanned out around it. Season lightly with salt and pepper.
▪ Add the vinaigrette to the still warm pan and scrape to combine with the pan juices. Dress each salad with the mignons. Pour a quarter of the pan juices and peppercorns over each salad and serve immediately. This is classy, delicious and almost free if you've been housekeeping properly.

Warm Salad of Sweetcorn and Chicken Livers

SALADE TIEDE BRESSANE

SERVES 4
Cooking time 5 minutes
INGREDIENTS
75 ml/4½ tbsp walnut oil
30 ml/2 tbsp butter
8 chicken livers
⅔ cup/100 g/¼ lb sweetcorn
1 frisée lettuce
1 head of radicchio (argula)
75 ml/4½ tbsp vinaigrette (*see* Vinaigrette)
Salt and pepper to taste

PREPARATION

Amalgamate the oil and butter in a frying pan (skillet) over a high heat. Toss in the chicken livers and sauté for 3 minutes on each side. Add the sweetcorn and remove the pan from the heat.

Arrange the frisée and the radicchio (argula) prettily on each plate and lightly season with the salt and pepper.

Add the vinaigrette to the still warm pan and scrape to combine with the pan juices. Dress each salad with two of the chicken livers, pour over half of the pan juices and the sweetcorn, and serve immediately.

Snails in their Shells with Garlic and Parsley Butter

ESCARGOTS A LA BOURGUIGNONNE

SERVES 4
(1 DOZEN EACH)

Cooking time 5–6 minutes

Oven temperature 200° C/
400°F/Gas 6

INGREDIENTS

225 g/½ lb butter

90 ml/5 tbsp finely chopped
garlic cloves

30 ml/2 tbsp chopped parsley

2 small chopped shallots

Salt and pepper to taste

48 prepared snails (see Cook's
Tips)

PREPARATION

▪ Well in advance of the meal, prepare the snails as
follows:
▪ Starve the live snails for 3 weeks or cover them for
24 hours with coarse salt.
▪ Wash with plenty of water and vinegar, then blanch for
10 minutes and then cool in cold water.
▪ Remove from the shells and cut off the black ends.
▪ Reboil for 3 to 4 hours in a court bouillon (see Court
Bouillon and Poaching Liquids). Drain and clean and dry
the shells thoroughly. Proceed with the rest of the recipe.
▪ Preheat the oven. Warm the butter very gently outside
the fridge. Beat it until soft, but do not let it melt.
▪ Add the garlic, the parsley, shallots, salt and pepper and
amalgamate thoroughly.
▪ Put the prepared snails in the shells and close the
openings with the butter.
▪ Bake the shells, openings uppermost, so the butter
does not leak, in a hot oven until the butter melts. Serve
instantly.

COOK'S TIPS

Nowadays, cleaned and
prepared snails are
usually sold in cans, often
in attractive, yuppy-style
packages with the shells
thrown in. Your cheapest
bet is to buy a couple or
three of these
presentation packs and
then save the shells.
They have a much longer
life than their occupants,
especially when the latter
are smothered in garlic.
However, if you do like
looking under stones or
patrolling highway
verges, there's nothing
to stop you doing the
thing properly.
Incidentally, the butter/
parsley/garlic
combination in this recipe
is not unreasonably
known as Snail Butter.
You can use it as a tasty
butter on many things,
meat and fish included.

Snails in Puff Pastry

ESCARGOTS A LA CHABLISIENNE EN FEUILLETE

SERVES 4

Total cooking time 30 minutes
Pastry 8–10 minutes

Oven temperature for the
pastry 175° C/350° F/Gas 4

INGREDIENTS

300 g/11 oz puff pastry (*see*
Pastry Making)

2 egg yolks

45 ml/3 tbsp finely chopped
shallots

300 ml/½ pt white wine –
which should be dry

½ cup/120 ml/4 fl oz meat
glaze (*see* Stocks and Glazes)
or 1 stock (bouillon) cube

24 prepared snails

¾ cup/175 g/6 oz snail butter

(For the last two ingredients
see Snails in Their Shells with
Garlic and Parsley Butter)

PREPARATION

▪ Preheat the oven. Roll out the pastry into a rectangle ¼ in/.5 cm thick and cut into 4 equal triangles.

▪ Brush the pastry with the egg yolks. Bake on a greased surface for 8–10 minutes or until a deep, golden brown. (Watch the pastry carefully; once it begins to brown it will burn very quickly.)

▪ As the pastry is cooking, set the shallots, white wine and meat glaze on a high heat and reduce by half. (If you are using a stock (bouillon) cube, reduce the wine and shallots on their own and add the cube at the end of the reduction.)

▪ As the stock is reducing – about 25 minutes – turn your attention back to the now-cooked pastry cases, which will have risen in cooking to about 1 in/2.5 cm in height. Cut them in half horizontally and scoop out any doughy pastry inside. You now have a top and a bottom.

▪ When the sauce is reduced, add the snails and heat through for 1 minute or so. Whisk in the snail butter with the pan off the heat. Do not reheat.

▪ Divide the mixture evenly between the four cases, spooning it into the bases, pop on the lids. Serve immediately.

Poached Sweetbreads in an Onion Case

RIS DE VEAU OU D'AGNEAU DANS SON HABIT D'OIGNON ROTI

SERVES 4

Cooking time 45 minutes

Oven temperature 175° C/ 350° F/Gas 4

INGREDIENTS

450 g/1¼ lb calves' or lambs' sweetbreads

2 large Spanish onions

60 ml/4 tbsp butter

100 g/¼ lb unsmoked bacon

100 g/¼ lb carrots

100 g/¼ lb turnip

225 g/½ lb mushrooms

60 ml/4 tbsp meat glaze (*see* Stocks and Glazes) or 1 stock (bouillon) cube

⅔ cup/150 ml/¼ pt white wine

Salt and pepper to taste

PREPARATION

▊ *Preheat the oven. Dice the sweetbreads – the lamb's, being much smaller, will require much less chopping – blanch in salted water for about 10 minutes, and then drain and set aside.*

▊ *Peel the onions and slice them into 2 equal halves. Prize out the inner cores leaving 4 bowl-shaped shells. These will form the edible containers for your breads.*

▊ *Chop the onion cores, bacon, carrots, turnip and mushrooms into small dice and sweat in the butter over a low heat until the root vegetables are almost cooked. Increase the heat and add the sweetbreads and cook until they begin to brown.*

▊ *Add the glaze or stock (bouillon) cube and the white wine. Reduce the heat to a simmer and cover.*

▊ *Cook the sweetbreads, vegetables, stock and wine together for about 30 minutes, or until the liquid has reduced to a coating consistency. While these are cooking, bake the onion shells for 5–6 minutes or until just soft. Remove and set aside.*

▊ *Season the sweetbreads, then spoon equal quantities of the poached mixture into each baked onion shell and serve immediately.*

COOK'S TIPS

Desist from asking which part of the animal the sweetbreads come from. Simply eat and enjoy. As Digby Anderson in the London *Spectator* has correctly advised us, anything that cannot profitably be eaten by mankind was thrown out thousands of years ago.

Mussels in White Wine, Parsley and Shallots

MOULES A LA MARINIERE

SERVES 6

Cooking time 5–6 minutes

INGREDIENTS

60 ml/4 tbsp butter

3 shallots, chopped finely

30 ml/2 tbsp chopped parsley

1 bay leaf

1 sprig thyme or 3 g/½ tsp dried thyme

7 Am pt/3.5 L/6 pt mussels, washed and brushed

⅔ cup/150 ml/¼ pt white wine

PREPARATION

▪ *Melt the butter in a casserole dish with a lid. Soften the shallots in the butter, then add the parsley, bay leaf and thyme. Allow to stew for 30 seconds or so.*

▪ *Add the mussels and the white wine and cover. The dish is cooked as soon as steam begins to force its way out of the pot. Serve immediately, or the mussels will toughen. Discard all those still closed.*

COOK'S TIPS

Do not salt this dish at all. And of course, the white wine you swallow with it should be dry as a bone and simple; try a dry white like Muscadet.

Frogs' Legs Sautéed with Parsley, Butter and Lemon

CUISSES DE GRENOUILLES SAUTEES FINES HERBES

SERVES 6
Cooking time 6–8 minutes
INGREDIENTS
½ cup/100 g/¼ lb butter
36 frogs' legs
30 ml/2 tbsp chopped parsley
Juice of 1 lemon
Salt and pepper to taste

PREPARATION

■ *Melt the butter in a frying pan (skillet) over high heat until foaming. Toss in the frogs' legs, reduce the heat to a medium flame and sauté for 6–8 minutes, turning occasionally and gently.*

■ *When the legs are cooked, toss with the chopped parsley, sprinkle with the lemon juice and serve them, if you can, from a pan that still has a sizzle in it.*

CHEF'S IRONY
Frogs' legs, that most quintessential of French dishes, are these days quintessentially Far Eastern, imported as they almost always are from Thailand and Bangladesh.

Leek Tart

TARTE AUX POIREAUX

SERVES 6
Cooking time 25–30 minutes
Oven temperature 200° C/ 400° F/Gas 6
INGREDIENTS
225 g/½ lb leeks – the white parts only
60 ml/4 tbsp butter
350 g/¾ lb unsweetened short-crust pastry (*see* Pastry Making)
2 eggs
1¼ cups/300 ml/½ pt milk
Salt and pepper to taste

PREPARATION

■ *Preheat the oven. Blanch the leeks for 5 minutes in unsalted boiling water. Drain.*

■ *Melt the butter in a frying pan (skillet) and slowly simmer the leeks until very tender – about 5 minutes. Allow the leeks to cool slightly.*

■ *Line a flan ring with the short-crust pastry. Spread the leeks evenly over the pastry.*

■ *Beat the eggs well and combine with the milk. Season with the salt and pepper and pour the egg milk over the leeks. Bake immediately and serve hot if you can.*

Fish and Fish Sauces

Marseilles Fish Stew

BOUILLABAISSE MARSEILLAISE

SERVES 6

Cooking time 1½ hours including preparation of fish soup

INGREDIENTS

5 Am pt/2.25 L/4 pt Provençal Fish Soup (*see* Provençal Fish Soup)

3 kg/6–7 lb various white fish (*see* Cook's Tips)

1¼ cups/300 ml/½ pt rouille (*see* Mayonnaise)

2 long French loaves

1 bulb garlic

225 g/½ lb grated Gruyère cheese

PREPARATION

■ Bring the fish soup to a rolling boil, then lower the heat until the liquid is restive but not too clamorous.

■ Add the white fish selection, cut into darnes or cutlets of roughly equal size: approximately 110 g/4 oz per piece. Do not fillet. Leave the bones in. Poach the fish pieces in the soup for 20–25 minutes.

■ As the fish is poaching, make, or retrieve from the fridge, the rouille and spoon into a serving dish (see Mayonnaise).

■ Slice the French bread and toast to taste.

■ Peel the garlic bulb and arrange the cloves, together with the grated Gruyère, in two small serving dishes.

■ Retrieve the fish pieces from the soup when cooked and arrange on a serving dish. Brush a little rouille over the fish.

■ Pour the soup into a tureen and serve with the fish, rouille, toast, garlic and cheese immediately. The peeled garlic is rubbed into the toast before the toast is dropped into the soup. The rouille and cheese are also dropped into the soup, either on or off the bread according to taste.

COOK'S TIPS AND INSIDE INFORMATION

All along the Provence coast of France, restaurants serve bouillabaisse to order, cooked in this fashion. The rouille, the toast, the cheese and the garlic will all have been prepared well in advance. The secret of bouillabaisse we have now succeeded in reducing to one task: the poaching of chunks of fish in a broth made from yet more chunks of fish, tomato and a handful of other humdrum ingredients. Purists argue about the right' fish to go into the soup. Let them. Though use white fish as oily, dark fish will spoil the soup's flavour. Serve with chilled rose.

Fresh Tuna Braised Bordelais Style

THON A LA BORDELAISE

SERVES 4

Cooking time 30 minutes

INGREDIENTS

90 ml/5 tbsp butter

60 ml/4 tbsp olive oil

450 g/1 lb fresh tuna

1 large onion

5 medium tomatoes

²⁄₃ cup/150 ml/¼ pt white wine

²⁄₃ cup/150 ml/¼ pt fish stock (*see* Stocks and Glazes)

225 g/½ lb mushrooms

Salt and pepper to taste

PREPARATION

■ *Amalgamate 60 ml/4 tbsp butter and the oil over a medium heat. Brown the fish in the oil and butter on both sides – about 2 minutes per side. Thinly slice the onion and add to the fish.*

■ *As the onion is cooking, deseed then dice the tomatoes. Add them to the mixture, together with the white wine and the fish stock. Bring the liquid to the boil, then lower the heat to a gentle simmer.*

■ *Cook the fish for 15 minutes, retrieve from the pan juices and set aside to keep warm.*

■ *With the remaining 30 ml/1 tbsp butter, fry the mushrooms until golden and add them to the pan juices. Turn up the heat and reduce by one-third. When the liquor is reduced, check the seasoning, pour over the tuna and serve immediately.*

Gratinée of Scallops

GRATINEE DE COQUILLES ST JACQUES

SERVES 6

Cooking time about
20 minutes

Oven temperature 200° C/
400° F/Gas 6

INGREDIENTS

²/₃ cup/150 g/5 oz butter

1 small onion

1 kg/2¼ lb scallops – out of
the shells and trimmed

1¼ cups/300 ml/½ pt dry
white wine

2½ cups/600 ml/1 pt
béchamel (see Béchamel)

2½ ml/½ tsp dry mustard

75 ml/4½ tbsp vermouth

Pinch of cayenne pepper

2 cups/100 g/¼ lb soft white
breadcrumbs

Salt and pepper to taste

PREPARATION

▌ Preheat the oven. Melt the butter over a low heat. Chop the onion very finely and soften it in the butter. Add the trimmed scallops to the pan. Pour in the wine, bring to the boil, then simmer gently for 1 minute.

▌ Remove the scallops from the broth and reserve. Boil the broth hard to reduce it to about a quarter of the volume.

▌ Slice the reserved scallops and fold them into one-half of the béchamel. Add the mustard, vermouth, cayenne, the reduced broth from the pan and salt and pepper to taste.

▌ Spoon the mixture into six ovenproof dishes or six cleaned scallop shells. Coat with the rest of the Béchamel.

▌ Melt the remaining butter and mix with the breadcrumbs. Sprinkle the crumbs over each portion and bake for 12–15 minutes in a hot oven.

COOK'S TIPS

Effectively, this recipe cooks the scallops twice. Why? Because when the scallops cook, they shrink and give off water. This water thins out any surrounding sauce, helping neither consistency nor flavour. Bear this in mind too if you wish to fry scallops. Poach them for a few seconds first.

CHEF'S ASIDE

Why Coquilles 'St Jacques'? It comes in via St Jacques of Spain, whose emblem the handsome shell happens to be. The terms *peigne* or *pélerine* (pilgrim) are equally acceptable.

Fillets of Sole in White Wine and Mushrooms

SOLE BONNE FEMME

SERVES 6

Cooking time 8–10 minutes

INGREDIENTS

1 small onion

3 Dover sole of about 450 g/1 lb each

⅔ cup/150 ml/¼ pt white wine

⅔ cup/150 ml/¼ pt fish stock (*see* Stocks and Glazes)

225 g/½ lb mushrooms

Juice of half a lemon

Hollandaise sauce made with 2 egg yolks and ¾ cup/170 g/6 oz butter (*see* Hollandaise)

Salt and pepper to taste

PREPARATION

▰ *Fillet the sole* (see *Boning*) *and chop the onion very finely.*

▰ *Place the sole fillets, onion, white wine and fish stock in a pan and poach over a gentle heat for about 5 minutes.*

▰ *Retrieve the sole fillets from the liquor, set aside, and reduce the pan juices until they are almost a glaze. Add the sliced mushrooms and poach for 2–3 minutes. Add the glazed mushrooms to the Hollandaise sauce. Season.*

▰ *Arrange the sole fillets on a heatproof dish, coat with the sauce and glaze for 2–3 minutes under the hottest grill (broiler) you can manage. Serve immediately.*

CHEF'S ASIDE

In Europe and Britain there are several different kinds of sole or, to put it another way, 'sole' is a name applied to several different types of fish. However, only one is truly fine and should be described in fishmongers and restaurants as simply sole – or very occasionally Dover sole. The rest are little better than plaice. In the United States, there are three major flat fish – flounder, halibut and a near relative to the Dover sole. Sometimes turbot too are available. Finally, and frivolously, does the name 'sole' have anything to do with shoes or footwear? The unlikely answer is yes. Small flat fish were originally called *solea* in Latin, as it was picturesquely thought that they might make suitable sandals for sea nymphs!

COOK'S TIPS

The lemon juice in the recipe is, of course, for the Hollandaise sauce, for which you will have found foolproof instructions earlier in this book. Two points, however. It is worth repeating once again that Hollandaise is not any kind of culinary impossibility for the amateur chef. It's easy. Secondly, its addition to fish sauces near the end of cooking is an absolutely standard and universal practice. So you're going to have to learn how to do it, aren't you?

Brochette of Prawns with Bay and Tarragon

BROCHETTE DE LANGOUSTINES À L'ESTRAGON

SERVES 6
Cooking time 10 minutes
INGREDIENTS
½ cup/100 g/4 oz butter
36 large shrimp, Dublin Bay prawns or langoustines
18 fresh bay leaves
60 ml/4 tbsp dried tarragon – double the quantity for fresh
Salt and cayenne pepper to taste
Juice of 2 lemons

PREPARATION

▪ Melt the butter over a gentle heat.
▪ Shell the fish and set aside the shells for later use (see *Shrimp Bisque*). Thread the fish onto skewers with one bay leaf per 2 prawns.
▪ Pour the melted butter over the fish, then sprinkle with the tarragon and the salt and cayenne pepper to taste. Grill (broil) for 5 minutes per side under a very high heat, pour over the lemon juice and serve.

COOK'S TIP

You may not naturally associate tarragon with fish. But with grills and broiled food, it is splendid.

Tomato and Browned Breadcrumbs Garnish

AU MISTRAL

SERVES 4

Cooking time about
20 minutes

Oven temperature 200° C/
400° F/Gas 6

INGREDIENTS

350 g/¾ lb tomatoes

⅔ cup/150 ml/¼ pt olive oil

225 g/½ lb sliced mushrooms

2 cloves chopped garlic

⅔ cup/150 ml/¼ pt white
wine

Salt and pepper to taste

¼ cup/15 g/½ oz fresh
breadcrumbs

PREPARATION

▊ *Preheat the oven. Peel and seed the tomatoes. Cut them into dice. Put the oil in a frying pan (skillet) over a high heat and add the tomatoes, sliced mushrooms and the chopped garlic. Sauté for 2–3 minutes.*
▊ *Add the white wine; salt and pepper to taste. Cook at a high heat for a further 2–3 minutes.*
▊ *Pour the sauce over the fish steaks in a deep baking dish (see The Fish) and sprinkle on the breadcrumbs. Bake in a hot oven for about 10 minutes or until the crumbs have crisped.*

THE FISH

Any fish which you can cut into reasonably sized, one-person steaks or cutlets will suit this method. Pre-cook the fish a little – and seal it – by browning each piece on both sides in hot oil or butter for 2 minutes before you sauce and bake.

White Butter Sauce

BEURRE BLANC

Cooking time 20–25 minutes

INGREDIENTS

2 cups/450 ml/¾ pt dry white wine

⅔ cup/150 ml/¼ pt white wine vinegar

1 medium onion

450 g/1 lb butter

Salt and pepper to taste

PREPARATION

▓ *Combine the white wine and the wine vinegar and chop the onion very finely.*

▓ *Set the wine, vinegar and onion over a very high heat and reduce until almost nothing remains. (This is literally true: the pan should contain nothing more than a shiny coating.)*

▓ *As the wine mixture reduces, work a little salt and pepper into the butter.*

▓ *Now employ an intermittent low heat: 30 seconds on, 30 seconds off. Using this technique, slowly whisk the butter into the reduced wine mixture. (Beat constantly with a whisk so the butter stays creamy. It must not melt.)*

COOK'S TIPS

Beurre blanc is another sauce that strikes terror into the amateur heart. If you follow the instructions patiently, you will not fail. Your sauce should achieve the consistency of thick cream. If too thick, beat a little more over low heat. If too thin – and unmelted – cool a little.
As to the fish, salmon or anything freshwater, poached. This sauce features in a dish called *Quenelles de Brochet au Beurre Blanc* (Pike Dumplings with White Butter Sauce). Make the dumplings the same way you make salmon mousse, but poach them in tablespoon shapes and serve hot.

Mussel and Prawn Sauce Dieppe Style
SAUCE DIEPPOISE

SERVES 6

Cooking time 20–25 minutes

INGREDIENTS

⅔ cup/150 ml/¼ pt dry white wine

⅔ cup/150 ml/¼ pt mussel cooking liquor (*see* Cook's Tip)

2½ cups/600 ml/1 pt white wine velouté (*see* Béchamels and Veloutés)

60 ml/4 tbsp butter

100 g/¼ lb cooked mussels

100 g/¼ lb cooked and peeled prawns (shrimp)

PREPARATION

▨ *Mix together the white wine and the mussel liquor. Set on a high heat and boil hard. Reduce the volume by one-half.*
▨ *Remove from the heat and whisk in the butter.*
▨ *Add the velouté, the mussels and the prawns (or shrimp) and reheat briefly.*

THE FISH

This is a light but chunky sauce. You could use it with any poached or grilled (broiled) flatfish to give these often bland fish a little extra boost, or with fine white fish such as Dover sole or American sole or turbot to emphasize their luxury. Not a sauce for anything oily. With grilled sardines, for example, it would be nearly as bad as custard.

COOK'S TIP

Mussel-cooking liquor is easily obtained: simply sweat the mussels in a closed pan and collect the juices that flow after they have opened. If the liquor is short, add a drop of water or white wine.

Red Wine, Mushroom and Onion Sauce Mâcon Style

A LA MACONNAISE/A LA BOURGUIGONNE

SERVES 6
Cooking time including the fish: about 30 minutes
INGREDIENTS
2 cups/450 ml/¾ pt red wine
¾ cup/175 g/6 oz butter
18 or so button (pearl) onions, peeled
Salt to taste
A pinch of sugar
225 g/½ lb mushrooms
60 ml/2 tbsp flour

PREPARATION

▪ Poach the fish in the red wine. Set aside and reserve the wine.

▪ Melt ¼ cup/50 g/2 oz of the butter over a medium heat and stir in the onions. Add salt to taste and the sugar.

▪ Just cover the onions with water and simmer until the liquid has evaporated – about 10 minutes – and the onions are agreeably glazed. Set aside.

▪ Sauté the mushrooms in ¼ cup/50 g/2 oz butter. Set aside.

▪ Place the reserved wine from the fish on a high heat and reduce by half.

▪ Mix the remaining ¼ cup/50 g/2 oz butter with the flour and beat into the wine on a low heat. (See Thickening Methods: Beurre Manié.) Combine the wine mixture with the onions and mushrooms and bring the mixture to the boil.

▪ Arrange the fish on some suitable platter, pour over the sauce and serve.

THE FISH

Fish in red wine? What sort of fish might that be? As a matter of fact, long-established recipes for this curiosity abound. You might use trout, either whole or in cutlets if it's a big sea trout. Likewise sole (flounder), salmon, too, and tuna. Bonito and snapper would fare equally well, as would red mullet or any well-fleshed river fish. Need I go on?

Brown Butter and Lemon Sauce

AU BEURRE NOISETTE

SERVES 4

Cooking time 5–7 minutes, including the fish

INGREDIENTS

½ cup/100 g/4 oz butter

Juice of half a lemon

A little chopped parsley

PREPARATION

▪ Melt the butter in a frying pan (skillet) over a high heat. Allow it to foam, then watch carefully until it begins to brown.

▪ Take the butter off the heat, toss in the lemon juice and allow the sizzle to subside a little. (Otherwise the butter will spit untidily.)

▪ Pour the mixture over the fish and sprinkle the parsley on top.

THE FISH

'Noisette' is a classic method for cooking fillets – always of non-oily fish – or whole fresh or seawater fish small enough to be cooked on top of the stove in around 10 minutes. In other words, flatfish of up to 450 g/1 lb in weight or conventionally shaped fish up to three-quarters of that weight are ideal. Larger whole fish are better baked, roasted or poached. There is a simple rule: the fish should be turned once only in the pan. If its size demands more turning to prevent burning beneath or excessive cooling above, it's too big.

Poultry Dishes

Chicken Breast in Walnut Oil Vinaigrette 45

Chicken in Red Wine, Cream and Mushrooms 46

Roast Chicken Stuffed with Bacon and Chicken Livers 47

Chicken in White Wine, Tomato and Mushrooms 48

Boned Roast Chicken with Tarragon 49

Turkey Breast with Olives, Peppers and Mushrooms 50

Périgord Preserved Duck 50

Roast Duck with Red Wine 51

Duck Braised with Turnips 52

Goose Braised with Onions, Chestnuts and Mushrooms 53

Chicken Breast in Walnut Oil Vinaigrette

SUPREMES DE POULET A LA VINAIGRETTE DE NOIX

SERVES 6

Cooking time 20 minutes

Preparation and cooking time 2¼ hours

Oven temperature 200° C/ 400° F/Gas 6

INGREDIENTS

6 chicken breasts, without the mignons (*see* Boning)

⅔ cup/150 ml/¼ pt walnut oil vinaigrette (*see* Vinaigrette)

30 ml/2 tbsp green peppercorns

60 ml/4 tbsp butter

30 ml/2 tbsp chopped fresh parsley

30 ml/2 tbsp chopped fresh tarragon — ¼ the quantity for dried

Coarsely ground salt and black pepper to taste

PREPARATION

▪ *Marinade the chicken breasts in the vinaigrette and the green peppercorns for 2 hours.*

▪ *When the chicken is ready to cook, preheat the oven. Melt the butter over a high heat on top of the stove. Seal each chicken breast in the butter — 15 seconds a side is ample.*

▪ *Arrange the breasts side by side in a baking dish — as tight a fit as possible — pour over the butter, cover and bake for 15 minutes or so.*

▪ *While the chicken is cooking, pour the vinaigrette and peppercorns into the pan that held the butter. Set on a very low heat, add the parsley and tarragon and stew the herbs very gently until the chicken is cooked.*

▪ *When the chicken is cooked, pour equal quantities of the herby vinaigrette over each breast. Sprinkle with the coarse salt and pepper and serve immediately.*

Chicken in Red Wine, Cream and Mushrooms

COQ AU VIN

Cooking time 30–40 minutes

Oven temperature 200° C/
400° F/Gas 6

INGREDIENTS

60 ml/4 tsp butter

5 ml/1 tsp olive oil

1 chicken, weighing about
1.4 kg/3 lb

225 g/½ lb button (pearl)
onions

340 g/¾ lb mushrooms

1 medium onion

1 bottle red wine as good as
you can afford to cook with
(*see* Cook's Tips)

⅔ cup/150 ml/¼ pt double
(heavy) cream

30 ml/2 tbsp chopped parsley

PREPARATION

■ *Preheat the oven. Melt the butter in a pan with the oil. Peel the onions and roughly chop the mushrooms.*
■ *Joint the chicken into 4 (see Boning) and brown over a medium heat in the oil and butter. When the pieces are brown, add the onions and the chopped mushrooms. Cook briefly together – a minute or so – then transfer to an oven-proof dish.*
■ *Cover the chicken and bake in the oven until tender – about 30 minutes.*
■ *Finely chop the onion and add it to the pan you cooked the chicken in – sweat but do not brown it.*
■ *Add the bottle of wine and boil hard until the volume is reduced by half. Add the cream and simmer until the sauce will coat the back of a spoon.*
■ *Separate the baked chicken from the mushroom and onion. Pour the sauce on top, then arrange the mushrooms, onions and chopped parsley on top of that. Serve.*

COOK'S TIPS

You should notice one thing about this recipe: coq au vin is NOT chicken braised in red wine. The sauce is made quite separately. Thus has it ever been, except in places that don't know what they're doing. The other interesting thing here is that the dish used to be called Coq au Chambertin. But insofar as the likes of us common folk no longer bathe in asses' milk, we no longer cook with Chambertin – one of the highest-priced Burgundies you can ever hope to find – or drink if it comes to that.

Roast Chicken Stuffed with Bacon and Chicken Livers

POULET GRAND-MERE

SERVES 4

Cooking time about
55 minutes

Oven temperature 200° C/
400° F/Gas 6

INGREDIENTS

60 ml/4 tbsp butter

100 g/¼ lb lean bacon

1 small onion

4 chicken livers

2 cups/100 g/¼ lb fresh
breadcrumbs

60 ml/4 tbsp chopped parsley

1 chicken, weighing about
1.4 kg/3 lb

⅔ cup/150 ml/¼ pt stock
(*see* Stocks and Glazes)

Salt and pepper to taste

PREPARATION

■ *Preheat the oven. Melt the butter over a medium heat. Chop the bacon and the onions and fry together until light brown.*

■ *Add the chicken liver, roughly chopped, and fry for a further 2–3 minutes. Stir in the breadcrumbs and the parsley.*

■ *Stuff the chicken with the mixture and roast in a covered casserole until tender – about 50 minutes – then remove it and set on a serving dish.*

■ *Set the roasting pan on a high heat and deglaze it with the stock, boiling hard for 3–4 minutes.*

■ *Season to taste with the salt and pepper, pour over and around the chicken and serve.*

COOK'S ASIDE

My editor asked me to find out why this dish was called, in French, Chicken Grandmother. 'Maybe someone's granny cooked it,' he said. Maybe.
I did make a few enquiries about the habits of French grandmothers, but drew a blank. But I think what the French are getting at is chicken, old-fashioned style.

Chicken in White Wine, Tomatoes and Mushrooms
POULET MARENGO

SERVES 4

Cooking time 1 hour

INGREDIENTS

1 chicken, weighing about 1.4 kg/3 lb

Salt and pepper to taste

Good ½ cup/50 g/2 oz plain (all-purpose) flour

60 ml/4 tbsp olive oil

½ cup/100 g/¼ lb butter

1¼ cups/300 ml/½ pt chicken stock (*see* Stocks and Glazes)

10 peeled button (pearl) onions

2 medium tomatoes, chopped and skinned

15 ml/1 tbsp tomato purée (paste)

3 cloves of garlic, crushed

100 g/¼ lb mushrooms

⅔ cup/150 ml/¼ pt white wine

30 ml/2 tbsp chopped parsley

PREPARATION

■ *Quarter the chicken, rub each piece with salt and pepper and dip them in the plain (all-purpose) flour.*
■ *Melt the oil and half the butter over a medium heat. Fry the chicken pieces until brown all over.*
■ *Add the chicken stock, the onions and the tomatoes. Stir in the tomato purée (paste) and the crushed garlic.*
■ *Cover the dish and simmer until the chicken is tender – about 40 minutes.*
■ *Meanwhile, slice the mushrooms and sauté in the remaining butter for 5 minutes or so. Add the white wine and bring to a brisk boil.*
■ *Add the mushroom sauce to the chicken mixture, garnish with the parsley and serve.*

COOK'S TIPS

People do say that Napoleon's chef whipped this one up for the boss just before the Battle of Marengo in 1800. Then again, others aver that it was a Paris restaurateur who concocted the name to celebrate the win – and to move a few more plates of chicken.

Boned Roast Chicken with Tarragon

POULET RÔTI DESOSSÉ A L'ESTRAGON

SERVES 6
Preparation time 2 hours
Cooking time 50 minutes
Oven temperature 180° C/ 375° F/Gas 5
INGREDIENTS
1 chicken, weighing about 1.4 kg/3 lb
1 medium onion
1 medium carrot
100 g/¼ lb celery
½ cup/100 g/¼ lb butter
Juice of 1 lemon
30 ml/2 tbsp dried tarragon – double the quantity for fresh
Salt to taste – preferably coarse rock salt

PREPARATION

▊ *Preheat the oven. Bone the chicken (see Boning). Roughly chop the onion, carrot and the celery.*

▊ *Place the chicken bones and the chopped vegetables in 5 cups/1.1 L/2 pt cold water. Bring to a brisk boil then lower the heat to a gentle simmer. (Begin this stock about an hour before you set the chicken to roast.)*

▊ *Meanwhile, gently soften the butter and then cream it with the lemon juice and tarragon.*

▊ *Lay the chicken on a flat surface, skin side down. Smear the butter into every nook and cranny.*

▊ *When the stock has been cooking for about an hour, seal the chicken with a skewer (see Boning) and put it in the oven, breast side down.*

▊ *Cook the stock for a further 30 minutes, then strain. Replace it on the heat and boil hard until the liquid has reduced by two-thirds. Set aside.*

▊ *15 minutes before it is ready, turn the chicken breast side up. Sprinkle it with a little rock salt.*

▊ *As soon as the breast has browned, remove the chicken and set it aside in a warm place. Deglaze the pan juices with the reduced stock, boiling hard for 2–3 minutes. Pour over the chicken and serve immediately.*

COOK'S ASIDES

Boned, a chicken of reasonable size will serve six, which makes excellent sense for simple dinner parties, families and portion-conscious restaurants. And as you see from the recipe, you also have the benefit of a very fresh stock made with the uncooked bones. Light red wine with this dish, or a heavy Californian, Australian or similar Chardonnay.

Turkey Breast with Olives, Peppers and Mushrooms

SUPREME DE DINDE A LA SAXE

SERVES 6

Cooking time 1½ hours or *see* Cook's Tips

Oven temperature 180° C/ 350° F/Gas 4

INGREDIENTS

½ cup/100 g/¼ lb butter

1 turkey breast, weighing about 1 kg/2.2 lb

225 g/½ lb red peppers

225 g/½ lb green peppers

225 g/½ lb mushrooms

1¼ cups/300 ml/½ pt velouté (*see* Béchamels and Veloutés)

½ cup/50 g/2 oz pitted black olives

Salt and pepper to taste

PREPARATION

▪ *Preheat the oven. Melt half the butter and baste the turkey breast. Roast the turkey breast in a medium oven for about 45 minutes. (See Cook's Tips.)*
▪ *Meanwhile, slice and de-seed the peppers and slice the mushrooms. Braise the peppers in the remaining butter over a gentle heat until they are soft – about 15 minutes – then remove with a slotted spoon and set aside. Braise the mushrooms in the butter and pepper juices for about five minutes.*
▪ *Replace the peppers in the pan and stir in the velouté. Set aside.*
▪ *Slice the olives very finely.*
▪ *When the turkey is ready, slice it diagonally through the breast into six escalopes.*
▪ *Return the mushrooms, pepper and velouté mixture to the heat and bring it to the boil. Season with the salt and pepper and pour an equal quantity over each turkey breast. Decorate with the finely sliced olives.*

COOK'S TIPS

In this dish, it is equally possible to use pre-roasted turkey. In other words, leftovers. This will appreciably shorten the cooking time and help to dispose of that increasingly problematic carcass in the fridge. As an extra garnish, you might also try slices of garlic sausage, warmed through in butter and layered on top of the breasts.

Périgord Preserved Duck

CONFIT DE CANARD

SERVES 4

Minimum cooking time 4 hours

Oven temperature 175° C/ 350° F/Gas 4

INGREDIENTS

1 duck, weighing about 2 kg/4½ lb

450 g/1 lb coarse rock salt

60 ml/4 tbsp dried thyme (double this quantity for fresh thyme)

CHEF'S ASIDE

As for the Périgord region itself, on all but the driest days, it gently reeks of damp earth and funghi – reasonable enough given the area's worldwide fame for mushrooms and truffles. Its other singular specialities are ducks, geese and the fattened livers therefrom.

PREPARATION

▪ *Preheat the oven. Joint the duck by removing the legs and the supremes, leaving on the wing bone up to the second joint (see Boning). Detach the mignons from the supremes and set aside for later use (see Warm Salad of Duck and Chicken Mignons). Trim all spare fat and over-lapping fatty skin from the 4 pieces.*
▪ *Combine the salt and the thyme, dredge over the duck thoroughly and set aside, covered, in a cool place for up to 24 hours (2 hours will do, just).*
▪ *Roughly chop the carcass and the fat trimmings and roast for 2 hours to render down the dripping, in which you will eventually simmer your duck. Strain the fat through a fine sieve (strainer) when rendering is complete and set aside.*

TO COMPLETE THE CONFIT
▪ *Retrieve the duck pieces, dry and de-salt thoroughly.*
▪ *Place in a loose-fitting pan and melt in the duck dripping. If the duck is not completely submerged, add lard until it is. Bring the pan to a brisk boil, cover, turn down the heat and bake for 2 hours or until the duck is very tender.*
▪ *Serve on a bed of red cabbage (see Chou Rouge à la Limousine).*

COOK'S TIPS

The browned, de-fatted duck carcass, along with a few sweated vegetables, could be the start of something big in the soup or stock department. So get cracking yourself or *see* Stocks and Glazes. Choose a red wine, naturally, and if it's the bank manager, a Cahors or Bergerac with the price left on. Critical prospective parents-in-law might be better softened up with a Grand Cru St Emilion. If southwestern France and you are oceans apart, the roughly corresponding wines would be, respectively, Shiraz (Syrah), Zinfandel and Cabernet Sauvigno

Roast Duck with Red Wine

CANARD A LA ROUENNAISE

SERVES 4

Cooking time 30 minutes

Oven temperature 220° C/ 425° F/Gas 7

INGREDIENTS

1 duckling, weighing about 1.4 kg/3 lb

1 medium onion

Salt and pepper to taste

²⁄₃ cup/150 ml/¼ pt red wine

PREPARATION

■ *Preheat the oven for several minutes, then roast the duck in the very hot oven for 15 – yes, 15 – minutes. It MUST be underdone.*

■ *Remove the duck from the oven and cut away the legs (see Boning). Roast the legs for a further 10 minutes.*

■ *Meanwhile, cut away the breasts and slice them in long, thin strips. Very finely chop the onion and sprinkle it on the bottom of a baking dish. Lay the strips of breast on top. Season to taste.*

■ *Now you must press the carcass a little – it will still be very pink – to collect as many juices as you can. Pour the juices onto the breasts and then pour over the red wine.*

■ *Retrieve the legs and arrange them on the dish with the breasts. Finish in the hot oven for 2–3 minutes. Serve on the same dish, straight from the heat, with the best red wine around.*

Duck Braised with Turnips

CANARD AUX NAVETS

SERVES 4
Cooking time 1½ hours
Oven temperature 180° C/ 350° F/Gas 4

INGREDIENTS

1 duckling, weighing about 1.4 kg/3 lb
60 ml/4 tbsp butter
⅔ cup/150 ml/¼ pt white wine
2 cups/450 ml/¾ pt meat stock (see Stocks and Glazes)
450 g/1 lb turnips
1 pinch of sugar
20 peeled button (pearl) onions
Salt and pepper to taste

PREPARATION

■ *Preheat the oven. Cut the duck into quarters (see Boning).*

■ *Melt the butter over a medium heat and brown the duck quarters on each side – about 2 minutes a side in a pan you have a lid for. Pour off the fat into a second pan, increase the heat and add the white wine and stock to the duck. Cover the dish and set it to bake.*

■ *If you have the inclination, you can carve your turnips into olive shapes. Otherwise, cut them into chunks, unless the turnips are baby ones. Braise them over a high heat for 3–4 minutes in the butter and duck juices, then set aside, with a pinch or two of sugar. Braise the peeled onions for the same time in the same juices.*

■ *Add the turnips and onions to the duck and finish cooking until tender. (The duck will take about 1 hour to cook. Add the turnips and onions when you're 30 minutes in.)*

■ *When everything is ready, remove the duck, turnips and onions and set aside in a warm place. Boil the juices down hard to a coating consistency. Season.*

■ *Arrange the duck and vegetables on a serving dish, pour over the sauce and enjoy it.*

Goose Braised with Onions, Chestnuts and Mushrooms

OIE A LA LYONNAISE

SERVES 8—10
Cooking time about 2½ hours
Oven temperatures 240° C/ 450° F/Gas 8 then 190° C/ 375° F/Gas 4
INGREDIENTS
1 goose, weighing about 3.6 kg/8 lb
60 ml/4 tbsp butter
20 peeled button (pearl) onions
⅔ cup/150 ml/¼ pt white wine
2 cups/450 ml/¾ pt strong meat stock (see Stocks and Glazes)
20 chestnuts, fresh (peeled and washed) or canned
225 g/½ lb mushrooms
Salt and pepper to taste

PREPARATION

▧ Preheat the oven for several minutes on the high setting. Brown the goose in the very hot oven for about 20 minutes.

▧ While the goose is cooking, melt the butter over a medium heat. Sauté the peeled onions until they are golden brown. Set them aside.

▧ Retrieve the goose from the oven and lower the temperature. Pour off all but a coating of fat from the goose dish.

▧ Add the white wine, the stock and the onions. Return to the oven and cook for 30 minutes.

▧ Add the chestnuts and mushrooms. Return the goose to the oven and cook for a further 1½ hours.

▧ Just before serving, lift the goose and the vegetables from the dish and arrange on a serving plate.

▧ Skim off the fat – you will find a good deal – from the cooking juices.

▧ Set the juices – still in the pan – on a high heat and boil very hard for 5 minutes.

▧ Check the seasoning, pour over the goose, and serve immediately.

Meat Dishes

How To Grill Meat

The feast is movable but allow 6–8 oz of meat per person

Cooking time 5–15 minutes

INGREDIENTS

The meat of your choice, cut into portions

60 ml/4 tbsp oil

Salt and pepper

PREPARATION

▌ Heat the grill (broiler) to its highest temperature.

▌ Rub oil, salt and pepper into the meat.

▌ Bring the meat to room temperature if you plan to serve it pink or rare – otherwise, the middle may still be cold when the exterior is browned.

▌ Grill or broil. Begin to test when both sides have been quickly sealed. Prod the meat with a finger and use these criteria:

▌ Lots of give in the meat. Deep craters do not spring back: near raw or bleu.

▌ Still plenty of give but the texture is springy: pink.

▌ Firm and browning in colour: medium.

▌ As black as your hat and twice as hard: well done (ruined!). It will be inferred from the last criterion that we do not much approve of well-done broiled or grilled meats. However, it may be that what the well-done brigades are really after is meat with a crisp coating. This is highly desirable but is better achieved by sautéeing – frying – than grilling (broiling). When sautéeing the points to remember are:

▌ First seal the meat at a very high heat in very hot fat.

▌ Then reduce the flame.

▌ Coat white meats with a little flour to help keep in the juices.

▌ Test for 'doneness' by the texture method.

COOK'S TIPS

There are 2 ways of testing the 'doneness' of a piece of grilled (broiled) meat, by texture (See Preparation) or by appearance.
Appearance comes into its own when the meat is placed on a barbecue or a griddle, methods in which the cooking takes place on the underside of the meat.

Wine Merchant's Fried Sirloin

ENTRECOTE MARCHAND DE VIN

SERVES 6

Cooking time 10–15 minutes

INGREDIENTS

½ cup/100 g/¼ lb butter

6 sirloin steaks, weighing about 175 g/6 oz

1¼ cups/300 ml/½ pt red wine

1 small onion, very finely chopped

Salt and pepper to taste

30 ml/2 tbsp chopped parsley

Juice of half a lemon

PREPARATION

■ Sauté the steaks to taste in half the butter, then set the steaks aside (see How to Grill Meat).
■ Pour three-quarters of the butter from the pan, turn up the heat and deglaze the pan with the red wine.
■ Bring the wine to a fierce boil, add the onion and season. Remove the pan from the heat.
■ Add the parsley, the lemon juice and whisk in the remaining butter.
■ Ladle over the steaks and serve.

Fillet of Beef with Sour Cream and Mustard

FILET DE BOEUF SAUTÉ STROGANOFF

SERVES 4

Cooking time 3–5 minutes

INGREDIENTS

575 g/1¼ lb beef fillet – the tail end will do perfectly

90 ml/6 tbsp butter

2 large onions

⅔ cup/150 ml/¾ pt heavily reduced meat stock or glaze (*see* Glazes)

⅔ cup/150 ml/¼ pt sour cream

5 ml/1 tsp French mustard

½ ml/½ tsp tomato purée (paste)

Juice of half a lemon

PREPARATION

■ *Trim the fillet carefully and cut into short thick strips.*
■ *Melt half the butter in a frying pan (skillet) over a very high heat. Toss in the strips of fillet and fry hard, tossing, for 1 minute.*
■ *Set the steaks aside and keep warm – preferably on a rack so you can collect the juices. Reserve the frying pan (skillet).*
■ *Chop the onions very finely in another pan, simmer them in the rest of the butter and, when soft, add the glaze and bring to the boil. Set aside.*
■ *Return the frying pan (skillet) to the heat and deglaze with the sour cream. Toss in the meat, the juices that have dripped from it, and the onions and glaze.*
■ *Stir in the mustard, tomato and lemon juice and reheat, without boiling, and serve.*

COOK'S ASIDE

This dish, together with Tournedos Rossini, is among the most maligned ever. When cooked properly, as above, it is delicious. But it can be made with nothing other than fillet steak. Anything else is not Stroganoff.
And why is Tournedos Rossini maligned? Easy. When did you ever eat this nugget of beef with a thick slice of black truffle (fresh) and *foie gras* (sautéed, not puréed)? This is the classic, correct presentation – as opposed to the usual slice of pâté and soggy fried bread usually offered.

Steak Tartare

BEEFSTEAK TARTARE

Portions given serve one
person. Preparation time
5–10 minutes

INGREDIENTS

175 g/6 oz fillet steak

Salt and pepper to taste

1 egg yolk

2 anchovy fillets

1 small onion, very finely
chopped

1 gherkin

PREPARATION

▮ *Trim the meat carefully of all fat and sinew, then mince
(grind) or very finely chop it. Season to taste with the salt
and pepper.*
▮ *Shape the raw ground steak on its serving plate in a flat
circle. Make an indentation in the middle. Place the egg
yolk in the hollow.*
▮ *Arrange the anchovy fillets and onion around the egg
and garnish the meat with the gherkin sliced into a fan
shape.*
▮ *Mix all the ingredients to taste at the table.*

COOK'S TIPS

There are one or two
more things you can add
to this utterly delicious
dish: Tabasco or
Worcestershire sauce,
capers, or even a dash of
vodka make piquant
additions. But be
gentle. This is a dish for
meat lovers, not vindaloo
or hot chilli addicts.

Beef Braised in Red Wine

BOEUF A LA BOURGUIGNONNE

SERVES 6
Cooking time 2½–3 hours
Oven temperature 180° C/ 350° F/Gas 4
INGREDIENTS
1 kg/2¼ lb beef topside or silverside
60 ml/4 tbsp lard or fat
60 ml/4 tbsp flour
2 cloves garlic
2½ cups/600 ml/1 pt red wine
Salt and pepper to taste
30 ml/2 tbsp dried mixed herbs
100 g/¼ lb lean bacon
1 large onion
15 ml/1 tbsp tomato purée (paste)
225 g/½ lb mushrooms

PREPARATION

▓ *Preheat the oven. Cut the meat into large cubes.*

▓ *Melt the fat over a medium heat and brown the meat, then reserve it on a plate. Set aside the pan and its juices.*

▓ *Lay the meat in a heavy casserole and sprinkle with the flour. Cook uncovered in the oven for 10 minutes.*

▓ *Add the garlic, red wine, salt and pepper and herbs. If the meat is still uncovered, top up with water, then cover and set to bake.*

▓ *While the meat is cooking, dice the bacon and fry briefly in the fat and meat juices. Roughly chop the onion and add to the bacon. When they are both well browned, add them to the meat.*

▓ *15 minutes before you are ready to serve the beef, stir in the purée (paste) and the chopped mushrooms.*

▓ *When the meat is cooked, check the seasoning once more and serve.*

Beef Braised with Tomatoes, Olives and Brandy

BOEUF EN DAUBE A LA MARSEILLAISE

SERVES 8

Marinade time 8 hours

Cooking time 3–4 hours

Oven temperature 180° C/ 350° F/Gas 4

INGREDIENTS

1.5 kg/3½ lb shoulder or rump steak

1¼ cups/300 ml/½ pt red wine

⅔ cup/150 ml/¼ pt brandy

225 g/½ lb carrots

225 g/½ lb onions

4 cloves of garlic, crushed

60 ml/4 tbsp mixed dried herbs

60 ml/4 tbsp cooking oil

225 g/½ lb fat bacon

Salt and pepper to taste

PREPARATION

▊ *Preheat the oven. Cut the meat into large cubes and marinate it overnight with the wine, brandy, sliced carrots and onions, the crushed garlic and the herbs. Pour the cooking oil over the top to seal the marinade.*
▊ *When you are ready to begin cooking, dice the bacon. Blanch it for 2–3 minutes in unsalted boiling water.*
▊ *Line the bottom of a casserole dish with the bacon. Add the meat, vegetables and marinade, making sure the meat is completely covered by the liquids.*
▊ *Seal the casserole very well and cook in a moderate oven until the beef is tender.*
▊ *Season with the salt and generous pepper and serve.*

Baked Pork Chops with Cheese and Ham

COTES DE PORC SAVOYARDES

SERVES 6

Cooking time 25 minutes

Oven temperature 190° C/ 375° F/Gas 5

INGREDIENTS

60 ml/4 tbsp butter

6 pork chops, each weighing about 175 g/6 oz

12 bay leaves – preferably fresh

6 thin slices of cooked ham

30 ml/2 tbsp chopped fresh sage – do not use dried

1 cup/100 g/4 oz grated Gruyère cheese

Pepper to taste

PREPARATION

▊ *Preheat the oven. Melt the butter over a medium heat and brown the chops for 5 minutes or so.*
▊ *Remove the chops from the pan, and pour the pan juices in a casserole dish. Line the dish with the bay leaves.*
▊ *Put the chops on top of the leaves and cover each chop with a slice of ham. Finely chop the sage and sprinkle it over the ham.*
▊ *Sprinkle the cheese over the sage, cover the casserole and bake for about 20 minutes.*
▊ *Season with the pepper before serving; you will not need salt.*

Grilled Lamb Cutlets with Minced Chicken

COTELETTES D'AGNEAU MADELON

SERVES 6

Cooking time about 25 minutes

Oven temperature 190° C/ 375° F/Gas 5

INGREDIENTS

60 ml/4 tbsp butter

12 lamb cutlets, weighing about 75 g/3 oz each

225 g/½ lb ground cooked chicken (or veal or turkey)

60 ml/4 tbsp béchamel (*see* Béchamel)

1 cup/50 g/2 oz fresh breadcrumbs

PREPARATION

▨ *Preheat the oven. Melt the butter over a medium heat and brown the cutlets – on one side only. Save the pan juices.*
▨ *Combine the ground meat with the béchamel (see Cook's Tips).*
▨ *Heap equal quantities of the meat mixture onto the raw side of the cutlets. Sprinkle over the breadcrumbs and pour the pan juices on top.*
▨ *Bake in a moderate oven for 20 minutes or until the crumbs are crisp and dark brown.*

COOK'S TIPS

This is a classic dish which makes a simple lamb chop much more interesting. And is something fresh to do with those intractable bits of chicken and turkey leftovers. It should also give you ideas: the ground meat need not be the usual chicken. It need not be meat at all, but chopped mushroom, or aubergine (eggplant), or peppers. Use your imagination.

Lamb Casserole

NAVARIN D'AGNEAU

SERVES 6

Cooking time 2½ hours

Oven temperature 170° C/
325° F/Gas 3

INGREDIENTS

1 boned shoulder of lamb,
weighing about 1 kg/2¼ lb

60 ml/4 tbsp butter or fat

60 ml/4 tbsp flour

3 cloves garlic

30 ml/2 tbsp dried.mixed
herbs – basil, marjoram,
rosemary, origano or chervil

30 ml/2 tbsp tomato purée
(paste)

24 button (pearl) onions

225 g/½ lb carrots

450 g/1 lb new (baby) potatoes

Salt and pepper to taste

PREPARATION

▨ Preheat the oven. Trim excess fat from the meat and cut into 2 in/4 cm cubes.
▨ Melt the butter or fat over a medium heat and brown the lamb pieces well.
▨ Pour off most of the fat and sprinkle with the flour; cook until it is golden.
▨ Crush and stir in the garlic; sauté briefly.
▨ Add water to cover the meat, the herbs and the tomato purée (paste), and bring to the boil.
▨ Cover the casserole and braise in a warm oven for 1 hour.
▨ Meanwhile, peel the onions and cut the carrots into batons. After the hour is up, add them to the casserole.
▨ Cook the casserole slowly for a further 45 minutes.
▨ Add the little potatoes (see Cook's Tips) and continue cooking everything together until the potatoes are tender.
▨ If necessary, skim the cooking liquor, season and serve.

COOK'S TIPS

If new or baby potatoes are unavailable, by all means use large ones. But it would be nice if you carved them a little into large olive shapes.

Lamb Cous-Cous
COUS-COUS A L'AGNEAU

Cooking time 2 hours

INGREDIENTS

60 ml/4 tbsp butter or lard

675 g/1½ lb neck or shoulder of lamb

1 large onion

225 g/½ lb carrots

225 g/½ lb turnip or swede (rutabaga)

100 g/¼ lb tomato purée (paste)

10 ml/2 tsp dried mint – double the quantity for fresh

1 medium can chickpeas (garbanzo beans) (*see* Cook's Tips)

Salt and cayenne pepper to taste

PREPARATION

▒ *Melt the butter or fat in a heavy saucepan. Cut the meat into large chunks, add to the butter and brown well.*
▒ *Roughly chop the onion, carrots, turnip or swede, add to the browning meat and cook until the onion begins to brown.*
▒ *Cover the contents of the pan with water, stir in the tomato purée (paste) and the mint, put the lid on the saucepan and simmer gently until the lamb is tender.*
▒ *Add salt and cayenne pepper – the broth should be distinctly spicy – and the chickpeas (see Cook's Tips).*

COOK'S TIPS

You may wish to use dried chickpeas (garbanzo beans). If so, soak them overnight in cold water and add them to the broth with the water.

Now, the dish itself. This casserole takes its name from the staple which accompanies it, a granulated form of semolina (*see* Cous-Cous The Quick Way). It is utterly delicious, particularly if:

▒ You serve with it a selection of other grilled (broiled) or roasted meats. Chicken, spicy sausage, lamb kebabs, would all be in keeping.

▒ You stew a few sultanas in some of the cooking juices and use them as a relish.

▒ You also make some harissa, the hot North African sauce with which you can tailor the spiciness of the broth to your own taste on your own plate. Simply mix tomato purée (paste) with broth skimmings and load it with enough cayenne pepper to lift the top of your skull off.

How did a dish hailing from North Africa find its way into French bistros and French life? The connection is colonial. Just as England, for example, has its Indian restaurants so France has its Moroccan Cous-Cous. And its Vietnamese cuisine, whilst we're on the subject.

What wine should you drink with cous-cous? By absolute preference, a fiery Moroccan red by the name of Sidi Brahim. Otherwise, any thick red.

Baked Beans with Potted Meats

CASSOULET

SERVES 4

Minimum cooking time
2 hours

Oven temperature 175° C/
350° F/Gas 4

INGREDIENTS

1 duck, weighing about
2 kg/4½ lb

450 g/1 lb coarse rock salt

60 ml/4 tbsp dried thyme –
double the quantity for fresh

2½ cups/600 ml/1 pt duck
dripping or lard

450 g/1 lb dried haricot beans

4 cloves garlic

100 g/¼ lb onions

60 ml/4 tbsp butter

⅔ cup/150 ml/¼ pt tomato
purée (paste)

Salt and pepper to taste

2 cups/100 g/4 oz fresh
breadcrumbs

PREPARATION

■ *Preheat the oven. Make 4 portions of preserved duck (see Perigord Preserved Duck).*
■ *Make 6 portions of White Beans with Garlic and Tomato (see recipe of the same name).*
■ *Layer the bottom of a casserole dish with half the beans.*
■ *Place the duck portions on top of the beans and add at least 60 ml/4 tbsp of the duck dripping. Cover the duck with the remaining beans.*
■ *Sprinkle the breadcrumbs thickly over the top and melt and trickle on a further 60 ml/4 tbsp of the dripping.*
■ *Bake in a moderate oven until all is piping hot and the breadcrumbs and dripping have formed a thick crust.*

COOK'S TIP

As you will have gathered, this is simply a composite dish made basically by adding two recipes together. But there is a little more to be said and it concerns what the French called *confits*. You know how to make *confit* of duck. The recipe is an easy one. But the French also make *confits* out of pork and goose and by exactly the same method: slow poaching in the appropriate dripping. Both these meats are regularly added to cassoulet, often together. In fact, at Castelnaudary in the Aude, the true home of this dish, they add salt pork, lean pork, garlic sausage, lamb *and* goose or duck. So you see, the world is pretty well your oyster here – mixed metaphors or not!

Garnished Sauerkraut Alsatian Style
CHOUCROUTE GARNIE

SERVES 6
Cooking time 2–2½ hours
Oven temperature 180° C/ 350° F/Gas 4

INGREDIENTS
1 kg/2¼ lb sauerkraut
175 g/6 oz bacon rinds
225 g/½ lb bacon
225 g/½ lb sausages firm-fleshed enough to boil
675 g/1½ lb pork steaks or chops (see Chefs Aside)
2 medium onions
2 cloves
2 medium carrots
30 ml/2 tbsp mixed dried herbs
½ bottle dry white wine
75 g/3 oz lard, pork, duck or goose fat
6 Frankfurter sausages

PREPARATION

▊ *Preheat the oven. Slice and wash the sauerkraut and squeeze it dry.*

▊ *Line the bottom of a casserole dish, big enough to hold all the ingredients, with the bacon rinds. Lay half the sauerkraut on top.*

▊ *Chop and blanch the bacon, and lay the bacon, sausages and pork on top of the sauerkraut.*

▊ *Stick each onion with a clove and add the cloved onions, carrots and herbs to the casserole.*

▊ *Top the meat and vegetables with the rest of the sauerkraut, add the white wine and the fat, and cover well. Braise in the oven for about 2 hours.*

▊ *Add the frankfurters: simply pop them on top of the sauerkraut and re-cover the casserole. Cook for a further 30 minutes.*

▊ *Before serving, remove the onions and the carrots. The sauerkraut should be heaped in its serving dish with the meats arranged around it. It should need no salt.*

CHEF'S ASIDE

The pork, is sometimes supplemented by duck, goose, or both.
How special a place in my memory choucroute garnie occupies! I can never forget one wintry Sunday lunch in Champagne, where my host Francis, *viticulteur* prepared for us the king and queen of choucroutes. Almost everyone at the meal was a champagne maker and as we worked our way through the mounds of goose, sausage, pork and cabbage, we were plied with bottle after unlabelled bottle, in all its guises: blanc de blancs, blanc de noirs, rosé, even still wine from the champagne grape. Then, quite suddenly, everything went black.

Pork Chops with Cream and Apples
COTES DE PORC A LA NORMANDE

SERVES 6

Cooking time 25 minutes

INGREDIENTS

60 ml/4 tbsp butter

6 pork chops, each weighing about 175 g/6 oz

450 g/1 lb cooking apples

Juice of 1 lemon

1¼ cups/300 ml/½ pt double (heavy) cream

Salt and pepper to taste

PREPARATION

▌ Melt the butter over a medium heat.
▌ Fry the chops until they are well cooked. Set aside in a warm place.
▌ Core and slice the apples and soften them in the pan juices. (Try to keep the slices whole – they will form the garnish.)
▌ When the apple is soft – about 5 minutes – remove it and set it aside with the pork.
▌ Turn the heat to high and add the lemon juice and cream. Bring the cream to a boil and reduce its volume by about one-third.
▌ Check the seasoning, then serve the chops with the sauce beneath them and the apple slices on top.

COOK'S TIP

A dash of Calvados with the apples is entirely permissible!

CHEF'S ASIDE

À la Normande invariably involves cream, although apples and consequently cider or Calvados also appear on the same billing. These are local Norman produce, alongside butter, cheeses, lamb – often salt-grazed – and pork. Genuine Norman fare is not for the faint-hearted.

Veal Cutlets with Herbs

CÔTES VEAU AUX FINES HERBES

SERVES 6
Cooking time 12–15 minutes
INGREDIENTS
100 g/¼ lb butter
6 veal cutlets, each weighing about 175 g/6 oz
⅔ cup/150 ml/¼ pt white wine
30 ml/2 tbsp chopped parsley tarragon and chervil
Salt and pepper to taste

PREPARATION

◻ Melt halt the butter over a medium heat.
◻ Fry the cutlets in the butter until cooked as you like them. Set them aside in a warm place.
◻ Turn up the heat and add the white wine to the cooking juices. Boil hard so the volume is reduced by about a half.
◻ Add the herbs.
◻ Off the heat, whisk the remaining butter into the pan.
◻ Season and serve the sauce poured over the cutlets.

Calves' Liver with Onions and White Wine

FOIE DE VEAU A LA LYONNAISE

SERVES 6
Cooking time 15 minutes
INGREDIENTS
90 ml/6 tbsp butter
3 large onions
3 cloves of garlic
6 slices calves' liver, each weighing about 100 g/4 oz
90 ml/5 tbsp white wine
Salt and pepper to taste

PREPARATION

◻ Melt 60 ml/4 tbsp of the butter over a medium heat.
◻ Finely slice the onions and crush the garlic. Sauté together until the onions are well browned. Lift out the onions with a slotted spoon and set aside.
◻ Melt the remaining butter and increase the heat to high.
◻ Sauté the calves liver – about 1 minute per side over a high heat for a pink result (see Grilling Cook's Tips). Remove and keep it warm.
◻ Deglaze the butter pan with the white wine and boil furiously for 30 seconds or so. Add the onions and stir.
◻ Pour over the calves' liver, season and serve immediately.

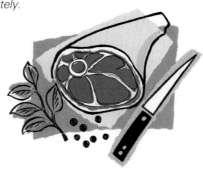

Game Dishes

Rabbit Casseroled in Red Wine 69

Braised Quails 70

Grilled Venison with Calvados 71

Partridge with Cabbage 72

Sautéed Pheasant in Cream Sauce 73

Pigeon with Onion, Bacon and Mushrooms 74

Hare with Mushrooms and White Wine 75

Rabbit Casseroled in Red Wine

GIBELOTTE DE LAPIN

SERVES 6

Cooking time 1½ hours

Oven temperature 170° C/
325° F/Gas 3

INGREDIENTS

½ cup/100 g/4 oz butter or lard

1 rabbit, weighing about
1.7 kg/4 lb

⅓ cup/40 g/1½ oz flour

2 cloves garlic, crushed

1 large finely chopped onion

2 cups/450 ml/¾ pt red wine

5 slices lean bacon

20 small or button (pearl)
onions

450 g/1 lb new (baby) potatoes
(*see* Cook's Tips)

Salt and pepper to taste

PREPARATION

◼ Melt half the butter, cut up the rabbit and brown it in the butter for about 5 minutes. Sprinkle the browning pieces with the flour, the crushed garlic and the finely chopped onion. Add the red wine and enough water to cover the meat. Braise the rabbit, covered, in a warm oven.

◼ While the rabbit is cooking, dice the bacon and peel the small onions. Brown them both in the remaining butter. Set aside.

◼ After 20 minutes, add the bacon and onions to the rabbit. Re-cover.

◼ As the rabbit, bacon and onions are cooking, peel the new potatoes. After a further 20 minutes, add these to the rabbit.

◼ Cook the casserole for another hour or so, season and serve.

COOK'S TIPS

No new or baby potatoes available? Use nicely shaped old ones, carving them a little if you have to.
And now to the subject of rabbit. There are practically as many recipes for rabbit as there are rabbits, which is saying something. The meat, devoid as it is of fat, is also extremely healthy and the flavour, though distinctive, is never strong. Eat and enjoy.

Braised Quails

CAILLES BONNE MAMAN

SERVES 6

Cooking time 15 minutes

INGREDIENTS

60 ml/4 tbsp butter

100 g/¼ lb onions

100 g/¼ lb celery

225 g/½ lb carrots

6 quails

⅔ cup/150 ml/¼ pt light stock (*see* Stocks & Glazes)

or

½ stock (bouillon) cube dissolved in ⅔ cup/150 ml/¼ pt hot water

Salt and pepper to taste (*see* Cook's Tips)

PREPARATION

▮ *Melt the butter over a medium heat.*
▮ *Julienne – or very finely slice – the onions, celery and carrots. Lower the heat and simmer the vegetables in the butter for 5 minutes.*
▮ *Add the quails, turn up the heat to seal the meat, then turn back to a simmer.*
▮ *Add the stock, cover and cook slowly for 10 minutes, then season to taste and serve.*

COOK'S TIPS

Watch the salt if you're using a stock (bouillon) cube; you may not need much. This dish can also be served cold, in which case a chilled Chardonnay would do the trick wine-wise. If the dish is hot, drink red.

Grilled Venison with Calvados

MEDAILLONS DE CHEVREUIL GRILLES AU CALVADOS

SERVES 6
Preparation time 30 minutes
Cooking time 10–12 minutes
INGREDIENTS
60 ml/4 tbsp butter
6 venison steaks cut from the saddle, weighing about 150 g/5 oz each
60 ml/4 tbsp Calvados
5 ml/1 tsp brown sugar
Juice of half a lemon
⅔ cup/150 ml/¼ pt meat stock (*see* Stocks & Glazes)
⅔ cup/150 ml/¼ pt double (heavy) cream
Salt and pepper to taste

PREPARATION

▪ *Bring the steaks to room temperature by leaving out of the fridge, covered, for about half an hour (see How To Grill Meat).*

▪ *Heat the butter in a frying pan (skillet) until foaming. Toss in the steaks and fry briskly for 2–3 minutes per side. Set aside, well covered, in a warm place.*

▪ *Add the Calvados to the pan – at a low/medium heat. As soon as the flames have subsided, add the sugar and the lemon juice.*

▪ *Now turn the heat up full and add the stock. As soon as the stock boils, whisk in the cream.*

▪ *At the same high heat, reduce the pan juices until the sauce is as thick as you like it. Check the seasoning, then serve the steaks at once. Pour half the sauce on the plates, place a steak on the sauce, and cover each steak with a bit of the remaining sauce.*

COOK'S ASIDES

The saddle steaks of venison – in beef terms the sirloins – are exceptionally tender and not at all high or gamy. But since they are so much less fatty – and healthier – than beef, they should be served pink. Furthermore, they should be accompanied by the most expensive Burgundy-style wine you can afford. This is a luxury dish, so give it the works.

Partridge with Cabbage

PERDREAUX AUX CHOUX

SERVES 6

Cooking time about 2 hours

Oven temperature 180° C/
350° F/Gas 4

INGREDIENTS

60 ml/4 tbsp lard or butter

3 partridges

1.4 kg/3 lb cabbage

4 slices lean bacon

350 g/¾ lb garlic sausage

2 medium carrots, peeled and
sliced

2 medium onions, peeled and
sliced

1¼ cups/300 ml/½ pt stock
(*see* Stocks and Glazes)

Salt and pepper to taste

PREPARATION

▌ *Preheat the oven. Melt the butter or lard in a large frying pan (skillet) over medium heat. Brown the partridges about 2–3 minutes per side over a high heat.*

▌ *Chop the cabbage and blanch it for 2–3 minutes in boiling water. Dice and blanch the bacon in the same water. Roughly chop the garlic sausage.*

▌ *In a large pan, bury the partridges in the cabbage. Add the bacon, the garlic sausage, the sliced carrots and onions. Pour over the stock and bring to a brisk boil.*

▌ *Now lower the heat, cover the saucepan and allow to simmer until the partridges are tender – about 1 hour for young birds.*

▌ *Remove the birds as soon as they are cooked and set aside in a warm place (see Cook's Tips).*

▌ *Check that all other ingredients are tender. If the cabbage mixture is still watery, strain all ingredients and set aside with the partridge.*

▌ *Reduce the remaining broth to the consistency of single cream, check the seasoning and serve the partridges on a serving dish surrounded by the cabbage, with the sauce poured over.*

COOK'S TIP

What are these warm places one hears so much about? They are usually low ovens. But make sure any food on 'hold' is well covered by lids or baking foil.

Sautéed Pheasant in Cream Sauce

FAISANS A LA CREME

SERVES 6

Cooking time 35–40 minutes

INGREDIENTS

½ cup/100 g/4 oz butter

2 young pheasants, each weighing about 1 kg/2¼ lb

2 cups/450 ml/¾ pt double (heavy) cream

60 ml/4 tbsp meat glaze (*see* Stocks & Glazes and Cook's Tips)

450 g/1 lb mushrooms

Salt and pepper to taste

PREPARATION

▊ *Melt half the butter in a frying pan (skillet) large enough to hold the pheasants.*

▊ *Quarter each pheasant (see Boning) and sauté, at first over a high heat. After 3–4 minutes' cooking, turn the pieces. Cook on for a further 3–4 minutes, then turn down the heat. (You should fry at a temperature hot enough to sizzle but not hot enough to burn the butter.)*

▊ *Turn the pieces again after 10 minutes, fry for a further 10 minutes, then set aside in a warm place (see Cook's Tips).*

▊ *Add the cream and the meat glaze to the pan juices and boil hard into a thick sauce. Season if necessary.*

▊ *As the cream is reducing, fry the mushrooms in the remaining butter.*

▊ *Arrange the pheasant pieces on a serving dish, pour over the sauce and garnish with the mushrooms.*

COOK'S TIPS

Ten minutes is all the cooking these birds will get. They are served pink and that's that. If the birds are old, however, they must be braised, in which case follow the recipe for Rabbit Casserole in Red Wine. Instead of a glaze, you might crumble a stock (bouillon) cube directly into the cream or, if you prefer, melt it first in a tiny amount of water. In this case, check the salinity of the cream before you reduce the sauce any further. Cream. One often hears it said that it will curdle (or something equally unappetizing) if boiled. But then one hears a lot of things, doesn't one?

Pigeon with Onion, Bacon and Mushrooms

PIGEONNEAUX A LA BOURGUIGNONNE

SERVES 4

Cooking time 50–60 minutes

Oven temperature 180° C/
350° F/Gas 4

INGREDIENTS

60 ml/4 tbsp butter

2 plump young pigeons

20 button (pearl) onions

2 slices lean bacon

²/₃ cup/150 ml/¼ pt white
wine – dry or sweet

²/₃ cup/150 ml/¼ pt meat or
game stock (*see* Stocks and
Glazes)

225 g/½ lb mushrooms

²/₃ cup/150 ml/¼ pt double
(heavy) cream

Salt and pepper to taste

PREPARATION

▪ Preheat the oven. Melt the butter over a high heat on top of the stove until foaming.
▪ Add the whole pigeons and reduce the heat to medium. Brown on each side for 1–2 minutes. Remove them from the pan and reserve.
▪ Peel the onions and cut the bacon into dice. Add them to the pan and fry both until light brown.
▪ Add the wine and the stock and replace the pigeons. Cover and braise in the oven for about 30 minutes.
▪ Meanwhile, wash and slice the mushrooms; after 30 minutes, add them to the cooking pigeons. (Take this opportunity to skim the cooking juices if you need to.)
▪ Cook the pigeons and sauce for a further 15 minutes, then take out the pigeons. Pour the cooking juices into a frying pan (skillet) on a very high heat. Add the double (heavy) cream and boil the sauce hard until it's as thick as you like it – which should take no more than 10 minutes. Check the seasoning, pour over the pigeons and serve pronto.

COOK'S TIP

Strange as it may seem, pigeons have a certain amount in common with squid. Both may be braised very slowly to produce a very tender result. But there is only one other alternative: extremely rapid cooking at a very high heat. Deep-fried, or blanched, squid rings cook in little more than 30 seconds. Brushed with oil and sautéed very hard, 30 seconds per side is not unreasonable for a pigeon breast when it enters the pan at room temperature and cut into a fan. Bear this in mind.

Hare with Mushrooms and White Wine

LIEVRE A LA FORESTIERE

SERVES 6
Cooking time 1 hour
Oven temperature 180° C/ 350° F/Gas 4
INGREDIENTS
60 ml/4 tbsp butter
1 hare, weighing about 1.5 kg/3½ lb
⅔ cup/150 ml/¼ pt white wine
1 sprig of thyme
1 pinch of chervil *or* marjoram *or* basil
2 bay leaves
3 cloves garlic
100 g/¼ lb lean bacon
450 g/1 lb mushrooms
Salt and pepper to taste

PREPARATION

■ *Preheat the oven. Melt the butter in a frying pan (skillet) on top of the stove until foaming.*
■ *Joint the hare and brown the pieces in the butter (see Boning).*
■ *Retrieve the hare and arrange in a casserole. Add the wine, the thyme, other herbs and bay leaves and the whole cloves of garlic. Cover and simmer in the oven for ¾ hour.*
■ *As the hare is cooking, fry the bacon – chopped – until crisp in the pan the hare was browned in. Set aside. Slice the mushrooms and cook them in the same pan until soft.*
■ *When the ¾ hour is up, add the bacon and mushrooms to the hare. Cook for a further 15 minutes, then season the juices and serve immediately.*

COOK'S TIP

Hare and rabbit may resemble each other from the outside but the meats are very different. Hare is much stronger than the pale, almost chicken-like flesh of the rabbit.

Vegetable Dishes

Braised Red Cabbage with Chestnuts

CHOU ROUGE À LA LIMOUSINE

SERVES 4
Cooking time 2 hours
Oven temperature 175° C/ 350° F/Gas 4
INGREDIENTS
1 kg/2¼ lb red cabbage
60 ml/4 tbsp butter or fat
450 g/1 lb shelled chestnuts
100 g/¼ lb brown sugar
1 meat stock (bouillon) cube dissolved in 1¼ cups/300 ml/ ½ pt water
or
1¼ cups/300 ml/½ pt stock (*see* Stocks and Glazes)
or
1¼ cups/300 ml/½ pt cider
Salt and pepper to taste

PREPARATION

▪ *Preheat the oven. Cut the red cabbage into fine strips.*
▪ *Line an ovenproof dish with the melted butter or fat.*
▪ *Add the cabbage, chestnuts, sugar, stock or cider. Cover and braise in the oven.*
▪ *Season with salt and pepper to taste when the cabbage is ready.*

COOK'S TIP

Red cabbage is a sturdy enough vegetable to re-heat without much appreciable quality loss. Just add a little more liquid first. Even water will do.

Green Lentils with Carrot, Onion and Garlic

LENTILLES A LA LORRAINE

SERVES 6
Cooking time about 1 hour
INGREDIENTS
450 g/1 lb green lentils
60 ml/4 tbsp butter
1 large onion
2 cloves garlic
1 medium carrot
45 ml/3 tbsp flour
1 pinch thyme, parsley, sage
Salt and pepper to taste

PREPARATION

▮ Wash the lentils thoroughly in cold water and then boil them until soft (see Cook's Tip). Set the lentils on one side, still in their pan.

▮ While the lentils are cooking, chop the onion, crush the garlic and slice the carrot into thin strips.

▮ In another saucepan melt the butter over a medium heat and add the onion, the garlic and the carrot. Cook the vegetables until the onions begin to brown, then stir in the flour and cook until golden.

▮ Now lift the lentils from their cooking juices and stir them into the saucepan with the vegetables. Gradually add small amounts of the lentil stock until you have a stew the consistency of thin cream.

▮ Season to taste with the herbs, salt and pepper and serve.

COOK'S TIP

We suggest green lentils for this dish because the green variety will only disintegrate after extreme provocation. If you are using red lentils, cook them carefully and remove them from the heat whilst they are still firm and in one piece.

French Beans with Garlic

HARICOTS VERTS A L'AIL

SERVES 6

Cooking time:
beans 10 minutes,
mange-touts 2 minutes

INGREDIENTS

675 g/1½ lb French beans
(or mange-touts [snow peas]

90 ml/4 tbsp butter

3 cloves garlic

Salt and pepper to taste

PREPARATION

▨ *Blanch the beans in boiling, salted water for 8 minutes or so. (The mange-touts will take only 30 seconds.)*
▨ *Melt the butter in a frying pan (skillet) over a low heat.*
▨ *Crush the garlic and add it to the butter.*
▨ *Turn the heat up high and, as soon as the garlic begins to spit, toss in the beans or the mange-touts (snow peas).*
▨ *Fry for a minute or so, dust with salt and pepper if necessary, and serve immediately.*

COOK'S TIP

Brussels sprouts can also
be cooked in this fashion.
Blanch them until cooked
but still firm – roughly
6–10 minutes depending
on their size.

Glazed Turnips

NAVETS GLACES

SERVES 6
Cooking time about 25 minutes
INGREDIENTS
1.4 kg/3 lb turnips
60 ml/4 tbsp butter
30 ml/2 tbsp sugar
salt

PREPARATION

▨ Cut the turnips into small pieces — preferably small olive shapes (see Cook's Tip).
▨ Melt the butter over a low heat.
▨ Add the turnips, the sugar and salt to taste. Pour in water until the vegetables are just covered.
▨ Boil without a lid until the liquid has evaporated completely. The turnips will be coated with a shiny glaze and taste excellent.

COOK'S TIP
In season, you may find baby turnips. Use these whole.

Fresh Peas with Lettuce, Onion and Parsley

PETITS POIS A LA FRANÇAISE

SERVES 4
Cooking time about 25 minutes
INGREDIENTS
60 ml/4 tbsp butter
4 cups/900 ml/1½ pt peas
1 small lettuce
8 small button (pearl) onions
30 ml/2 tbsp chopped parsley – fresh
1 pinch of sugar
5 ml/1 tsp plain (all-purpose) flour
Salt and pepper to taste

PREPARATION

▨ *Melt the butter in a saucepan and add the peas.*
▨ *Shred the lettuce finely, peel but do not chop the onions. Add them to the peas, together with the parsley.*
▨ *Reduce the heat to a very gentle simmer, then stir in the sugar and flour. Add water until the peas are just covered. Season and cover.*
▨ *Cook gently for about 20 minutes, or until both the peas and onions are tender. The consistency should be that of single (light) cream.*

Braised Chicory
ENDIVES BRAISÉES

SERVES 6

Cooking time 1 hour

Oven temperature 170° C/
325° F/Gas 2

INGREDIENTS

900 g/2 lb chicory (Belgian
endive)

60 ml/4 tbsp butter

Juice of 1 lemon

Salt and pepper to taste

⅔ cup/150 ml/¼ pt meat
velouté (*see* Béchamels and
Veloutés)

PREPARATION

▊ *Preheat the oven. Blanch the chicory (endive) for 5 minutes in lightly boiling water on top of the stove. Drain.*
▊ *Baste a casserole dish with the melted butter and place the chicory in one layer in it.*
▊ *Pour the lemon juice over and season with salt and pepper to taste, then add the velouté.*
▊ *Cover and bake for about 50 minutes.*

CHEF'S ASIDE

Endive – or chicory – may
well prove a source of
confusion to the unwary.
It works like this:
French
ENDIVE
Chicoré
English
CHICORY
Endive
American
BELGIAN ENDIVE
Chicory
What is it?
SLIM, PALE GREEN TO WHITE
BULBS
Frizzy, lettuce-like salad
vegetable

Perhaps as a result of this
somewhat odd inversion,
'frisée' is now being
widely used of the
lettuce-like vegetable,
both in France and in
English-speaking
countries.

White Haricot Beans with Garlic and Tomato
HARICOTS BLANCS A LA BRETONNE

Preparation time 2 hours

Cooking time 1½–2 hours

INGREDIENTS

450 g/1 lb dried haricot beans

4 cloves garlic

100 g/¼ lb onions

60 ml/4 tbsp butter

⅔ cup/150 ml/¼ pt tomato
purée (paste)

Salt and pepper to taste

PREPARATION

▊ *Soak the dried beans in cold water for two hours. Drain.*
▊ *Crush the garlic cloves and roughly slice the onion, soften them in the butter.*
▊ *Stir in the drained beans, the tomato purée (paste) and enough water to cover the beans by 1 in/2 cm or so. Bring the mixture to the boil then lower the heat to a gentle simmer. (Check the water level during cooking. Top up to the original level half-way through if necessary.)*
▊ *Season to taste with salt and pepper when the beans are tender.*

COOK'S TIPS

This is a splendid
accompaniment to leg of
lamb. It can also form the
basis for Castelnaudary's
glory (*see* Baked Beans
with Potted meats
[Cassoulet]).

Braised Chestnuts with Thyme and Bacon

MARRONS BRAISÉS AU LARD

SERVES 6
Cooking time 20 minutes
INGREDIENTS
450 g/1 lb fresh or canned chestnuts
60 ml/4 tbsp butter
1 large onion
100 g/¼ lb lean bacon
1 medium carrot
1 sprig fresh thyme – or 2 pinches of dried
⅔ cup/150 ml/¼ pt stock (*see* Stocks and Glazes) or 1 stock (bouillon) cube
Salt and pepper to taste

PREPARATION

■ *If the chestnuts are fresh, peel them (see Cook's Tip). Otherwise, wash the canned ones carefully – they have probably been preserved in brine.*

■ *Melt the butter in a frying pan (skillet). Dice the onion finely and brown slightly in the butter.*

■ *Dice both the bacon and the carrot and add to the onion and butter. Follow with the chestnuts, the thyme and the stock or the stock cube and ⅔ cup/150 ml/¼ pt water.*

■ *Cover the pan and cook slowly for 15 minutes or so. Check the seasoning and serve.*

COOK'S TIP

Chestnuts can be obstinate to peel. To make it easier, score the nuts with a sharp knife, drop them in fat which is hot but not hot enough to fry them immediately, and cook for about 5 minutes. The skins will begin to open of their own accord, when they can easily be peeled off. Clean the oil off the chestnuts before you cook them.

Aubergines (Eggplants) Stuffed with Garlic and Tomato

AUBERGINES FARCIES A LA PROVENÇALE

SERVES 6

Cooking time 15 minutes

Oven temperature 200° C/
400° F/Gas 6

INGREDIENTS

1 kg/2¼ lb aubergines
(eggplants)

⅔ cup/150 ml/¼ pt olive oil

1 kg/2¼ lb tomatoes

4 cloves of garlic

60 ml/2 tbsp chopped parsley

Salt and pepper to taste

PREPARATION

■ Preheat the oven. Slice the aubergines (eggplants) in half lengthways.

■ Fry them in the oil – about 2 minutes per side at a high heat. Lift out the aubergines (eggplants), drain and allow to cool slightly.

■ Deseed and dice the tomatoes and fry in the oil.

■ Scoop out the aubergine (eggplant) flesh, leaving a shell about ¼ in/.5 cm thick. Reserve the shells.

■ Crush the garlic and add, with the chopped flesh of the aubergines (eggplants), to the tomatoes. Stir in the chopped parsley and season to taste with the salt and pepper.

■ Cook over a medium heat for about 5 minutes. Then scoop out the mixture with a slotted spoon, pressing out any excess oil, and fill each of the aubergine (eggplant) halves with some of it. Bake until the cases and filling are hot all the way through.

Stuffed Baked Potatoes

POMMES FARCIES AU FOUR

SERVES 6

Cooking time 70 minutes approximately

Oven temperature 200° C/ 400° F/Gas 6

INGREDIENTS

6 clean, dry potatoes, each weighing about 150 g/5 oz

⅔ cup/150 ml/¼ pt double (heavy) cream, mixed with 75 ml/4½ tbsp milk

60 ml/4 tbsp butter

½ cup/50 g/2 oz grated Gruyère cheese

Salt and pepper seasoning to taste

PREPARATION

▮ Bake the potatoes in their skins for about 1 hour, or until almost cooked. Slice in half lengthways.

▮ Scoop out the flesh with care, leaving a shell of skin and potato about ¼ in/.5 cm thick. Replace the shells in the oven for about 10 minutes or until crisp.

▮ As the shells are crisping, mash the potato flesh with the cream, milk, butter and half the cheese. Season with salt and pepper to taste.

▮ Remove the shells from the oven and fill with the mixture. Sprinkle the remaining cheese over the stuffed potatoes.

▮ Replace in the oven for about 10 minutes or until the cheese has melted and browned.

Matchstick Potatoes

POMMES ALLUMETTES

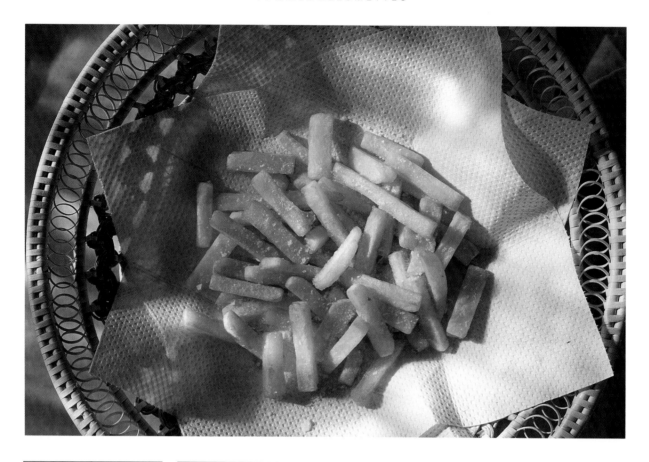

SERVES 6
Cooking time 6–7 minutes
INGREDIENTS
1.1 L/2 pt cooking oil
1 kg/2¼ lb potatoes
Salt

PREPARATION

■ *Heat the oil to 190° C/375° F.*
■ *Peel the potatoes and slice into fine batons, about 2 in/5 cm long and ¼ in/.5 cm square.*
■ *Fry in the very hot oil, pat free of grease and serve immediately, salted to taste.*

COOK'S TIPS

There are two things to remember about deep frying:
■ Judge the batches of food carefully. Too large a batch will push down the oil temperature and get you a soggy result. There is no such thing as too small a batch.
■ Since the water content of vegetables is high and is released by frying, the level of the oil may rise. Fry in a basket and lift the food out if the level goes critical. Pop it back when the level drops.

Pot Roast Potatoes

POMMES A LA BOULANGERE

SERVES 6
Cooking time 35–40 minutes
Oven temperature 200° C/ 400° F/Gas 6
INGREDIENTS
100 g/¼ lb good fat
1 kg/2¼ lb potatoes
225 g/½ lb onions
1.1 L/2 pt bouillon (*see* Court Bouillons and Poaching Liquids)
Salt to taste

PREPARATION

▢ Preheat the oven. Grease a baking dish well with the fat or lard.

▢ Cut the potatoes in thick, round slices and chop the onions roughly.

▢ Fill the dish with the potatoes and onions and pour over the bouillon.

▢ Bake in a hot oven until the bouillon has completely evaporated and the potatoes are tender.

Sautéed Potatoes with Onions

POMMES A LA LYONNAISE

SERVES 6

Cooking time 30–40 minutes

INGREDIENTS

1 kg/2½ lb potatoes

100 g/¼ lb butter

225 g/½ lb onions

30 ml/2 tbsp chopped parsley

Salt and pepper to taste

PREPARATION

■ Boil the potatoes in their jackets until tender. Drain, peel and slice them.
■ Gently fry the potatoes until brown in 60 ml/2 tbsp butter.
■ As the potatoes are cooking, slice the onions finely and fry them in the remaining butter until golden brown.
■ Just before serving, combine the potatoes and onions and fry briefly together – about 3–4 minutes. Season with the salt and pepper, sprinkle with parsley and serve.

Baked Potatoes with Tomato and Paprika
POMMES A LA HONGROISE

SERVES 6

Cooking time about 30 minutes

Oven temperature 190° C/ 375° F/Gas 5

INGREDIENTS

60 ml/4 tbsp butter

2 medium onions

1 kg/2¼ lb potatoes

45 ml/3 tbsp tomato purée (paste)

1¼ cups/300 ml/½ pt bouillon (*see* Courts Bouillons and Poaching Liquids)

30 ml/2 tbsp paprika

Salt to taste

PREPARATION

▌ *Preheat the oven. Melt the butter in a flameproof baking dish.*
▌ *Peel and slice the onions and sauté until golden. Peel and slice the potatoes and add them to the onions.*
▌ *Mix in the tomato purée (paste), and add the bouillon and the paprika.*
▌ *Salt the mixture to taste and bake uncovered until the potatoes are tender.*

Baked Potatoes with Garlic, Cheese and Milk

GRATIN DAUPHINOIS

SERVES 6

Cooking time 40–50 minutes

Oven temperature 180° C/
350° F/Gas 4

INGREDIENTS

30 ml/2 tbsp butter

2 cloves garlic

1 kg/2¼ lb potatoes

Salt and pepper to taste

Nutmeg to taste

1 egg

1¼ cups/300 ml/½ pt milk

¾ cup/75 g/3 oz grated
Gruyère cheese

PREPARATION

▪ *Preheat the oven. Thickly butter a baking dish, then sprinkle in the crushed garlic.*
▪ *Layer the dish with thin slices of potato cut in rounds and season with the salt, pepper and nutmeg.*
▪ *Beat the egg and mix with the milk and pour the mixture over the potatoes so they are all covered.*
▪ *Sprinkle the grated cheese on top. Bake until the potatoes are tender and the crust is firm and golden.*

Baked Potatoes with Onions and Cheese

GRATIN A LA SAVOYARDE

SERVES 6

Cooking time 35–40 minutes

Oven temperature 190° C/
375° F/Gas 5

INGREDIENTS

90 ml/6 tbsp butter

175 g/6 oz onions

1 kg/2½ lb potatoes

100 g/¼ lb Gruyère cheese

300 ml/½ lb bouillon (*see*
Courts Bouillons and
Poaching Liquids)

Salt to taste

PREPARATION

▮ *Melt the butter over a low heat.*
▮ *Slice the onions and sweat them in the butter until soft.*
▮ *Slice the potatoes and add them to the onions.*
▮ *Slice the cheese thinly and mix with the onion and potato.*
▮ *Arrange the mixture in a baking dish and half cover the contents with the bouillon. Season and bake until the potatoes are tender.*

Egg and Grain Dishes

Herb Omelet

OMELETTE AUX FINES HERBES

SERVES 1

Cooking time 3–4 minutes

INGREDIENTS

30 ml/2 tbsp butter

2 eggs

15 ml/1 tbsp chopped fresh parsley, chives, tarragon, chervil

Salt and pepper to taste

PREPARATION

■ Melt the butter until it foams (see *Cook's Tips*).
■ Lightly beat the eggs – just enough to mix whites and yolks. Stir in a teaspoon of cold water.
■ Pour the egg mixture into the foaming butter. Tilt the pan this way and that so the mixture spreads evenly.
■ Loosen the edges as they begin to set, then lower the heat and sprinkle the herbs on the egg. It should still be moist.
■ Fold one edge of the omelet into the middle. Fold the other over and slide it out of its pan. Sprinkle with salt and pepper and serve.

CHEF'S ASIDE

Some of you wordsmiths out there may be wondering: but why is it called an omelet? Here are a few possibilities for you to toy with:
■ An elision of *oeufs meslette*, or mixed eggs.
■ From the old French *alumette*, a tin plate.

COOK'S TIPS

People do say that an omelet pan should never be washed but simply wiped dry. This is not true of pans with non-stick surfaces.
How do you prove a pan, anyway? Simply line it with salt and set on a very high heat for a good ten minutes. The salt will lift off impurities and thoroughly dry the surface. Tip the salt away – make sure absolutely none remains – and pour in oil up to ¼ in/.5 cm Return the pan to the heat until the oil smokes. Pour away the oil, wipe with tissue and carry on. Once washed, remember, the pan will need reproving.

Baked Eggs with Red Wine

OEUFS EN COCOTTE AU VIN ROUGE

SERVES 1
Cooking time 5 minutes
Oven temperature 200° C/ 400° F/Gas 6
INGREDIENTS
30 ml/2 tbsp butter
60 ml/4 tbsp red wine
2 eggs
Salt and pepper to taste

PREPARATION

■ *Preheat the oven. Melt the butter over a low heat on top of the stove and mix in the wine.*
■ *Pour the hot mixture into a ramekin and break the eggs into it.*
■ *Set the ramekin in boiling water for 2 minutes.*
■ *Finish the cooking in the oven so the egg will glaze.*
■ *Season and serve.*

Baked Cream Cheese and Eggs with Ham

PAIN MOULE A LA FERMIERE

SERVES 2

Cooking time 15 minutes

Oven temperature 190° C/
375° F/Gas 5

INGREDIENTS

225 g/½ lb cream cheese

60 ml/4 tbsp butter

2 slices cooked ham

4 eggs

60 ml/4 tbsp double (heavy)
cream

Salt and cayenne pepper to
taste

PREPARATION

▢ Preheat the oven. Squeeze out the cream cheese in a cloth to dry it.
▢ Beat the cheese very thoroughly until creamy, then soften the butter and whip it into the cheese.
▢ Cut the ham into very small dice and lightly beat the eggs.
▢ Fold the ham and eggs into the cheese mixture, and season with the salt and cayenne.
▢ Poach uncovered in a water bath in the preheated oven for about 15 minutes, or until set (see Salmon Mousse Chaud-Froid for poaching instructions).

Fried Eggs with Gravy and Herbs

OEUFS AU PLAT CHARTRES

Cooking time 4–5 minutes

Oven temperature 200° C/
400° F/Gas 6

INGREDIENTS

60 ml/4 tbsp roast meat gravy
or strong stock (*see* Stocks
and Glazes)

A pinch dried tarragon

2 eggs

Salt and pepper to taste

PREPARATION

■ *Preheat the oven. Pour the gravy into a small baking dish and add the tarragon.*
■ *Break the eggs into the dish, taking care to keep the yolks whole.*
■ *Season with salt and pepper and bake until set.*

Fried Eggs with Peppers and Ham

PIPERADE

SERVES 2
Cooking time 20 minutes
INGREDIENTS
60 ml/4 tbsp butter
1 small onion
1 green pepper
1 red pepper
2 slices cooked ham
Pinch cayenne pepper
Salt to taste
3 eggs

PREPARATION

▪ Melt the butter in a frying pan (skillet) over a medium heat until foaming gently.

▪ Finely slice the onion and the peppers.

▪ Add the onion to the butter and cook until soft but not browned, then stir in the peppers and cook until soft — about 10 minutes.

▪ As the peppers are cooking, cut the ham into small dice.

▪ When the vegetables are cooked, season them, scrape them into a bowl and set aside in a warm place.

▪ Brown the ham in the frying pan (skillet), then lift out the ham pieces with a slotted spoon and add them to the vegetables in the bowl.

▪ Return the pan to the heat. Whisk up the eggs and cook them in the vegetable juices, omelet style.

▪ As soon as a crust has formed, add the vegetable and ham mixture and whisk it slightly into the egg.

▪ Serve immediately, garnished with the browned ham.

French Scrambled Eggs

OEUFS BROUILLES

SERVES 2

Cooking time 5–6 minutes

INGREDIENTS

60 ml/4 tbsp butter

4 eggs

60 ml/4 tbsp double (heavy) cream

Salt and pepper to taste

PREPARATION

■ *Melt the butter in a bowl standing in boiling water.*
■ *Break the eggs into the bowl and add the cream and seasoning (see Cook's Tips).*
■ *Stir the eggs briskly until the mixture begins to stiffen.*
■ *The finished result should remain soft and creamy and not, on any account, boarding-house granular.*

COOK'S TIPS

As you see, there is a proper way to make scrambled eggs and this is it. There are also numerous classic recipes which involve eggs cooked in this fashion, most of which involve adding other things. Here are some ideas for you to toy with:
■ Aux Champignons – with mushrooms.
■ Chasseur – with sautéed chicken livers and mushrooms.
■ À la Clamart – with peas à la Francaise (*see* Fresh Peas with Lettuce, Onion and Parsley)
■ Aux Fonds d'Artichauts – with artichoke hearts.
■ À la Normande – with oysters or mussels.

Noodles with Butter and Cheese
NOUILLES A L'ALSACIENNE

SERVES 6
Cooking time 8–10 minutes
INGREDIENTS
450 g/1 lb fresh noodles (*see* Cook's Tips)
60 ml/4 tbsp butter
¾ cup/75 g/3 oz grated cheese
Salt to taste

PREPARATION

■ Cook the noodles in plenty of salted water for 5 minutes or so. Drain. Pinch off 3 or 4 strands and set the rest aside. Dice the few strands finely and fry them in the butter until golden. Reserve.

■ Immediately before serving, toss the main batch of noodles into the butter and fry briskly, stirring in the cheese. Serve the noodles as soon as they are hot and the cheese has melted.

■ Toss the crisped noddle trimmings on top as a garnish.

COOK'S TIPS

Where will you get your pasta from? Buying it from delicatessens, supermarkets and pasta shops is now easy. Here is the more difficult method. It involves making it yourself.
Take:
450 g/1 lb strong white flour
2 eggs
A pinch of salt

Make a firm dough with the flour, eggs and salt. Let it rest in a damp cloth for 2 hours. On a floured board, roll the dough out as thinly as you can. Slice it into thin strips. After practice this may well become as easy as buying the fresh stuff from your smart local store.

Cous-Cous the Quick Way

COUS-COUS RAPIDE

Cooking time 10 minutes

INGREDIENTS

½ cup/100 g/¼ lb butter

225 g/½ lb cous-cous

Salt to taste

■ *Melt the butter in a frying pan (skillet) over a low heat.*
■ *Add the cous-cous and about 3 times its own volume of water. Stir and add salt to taste.*
■ *Turn the heat down to very low and allow the cous-cous to stand. In about 10 minutes, when the cereal holds the shape of a spoon pushed through it, the grains will be cooked.*

There exists, in the literature of cous-cous, the near-mythical Moroccan *cous-cousière*, a gadget which is clamped over the broth which accompanies the cereal (*see* Lamb Cous-Cous). The grains are thus steamed so they absorb the subtle flavours – largely mint, chilli and tomato – of the sauce below. The fact that this broth is promptly poured all over these grains during the eating process – a hugely enjoyable one in the case of this particular dish – seems rather to cancel the advantage of this piece of gastronomic gentility. So we offer you 'Le Moyen Rapide': it's the one the French use.

Rice with Peas and Ham

RIZ A LA GRECQUE

SERVES 6

Cooking time 30 minutes

Oven temperature 180° C/
350° F/Gas 4

INGREDIENTS

60 ml/4 tbsp butter

1 small onion

1 kg/2¼ lb rice

6 cups/1.2 L/2¼ pt bouillon
(*see* Court Bouillons and
Poaching Liquids)

2 cloves garlic

2 bay leaves

Salt

100 g/¼ lb cooked ham

100 g/¼ lb shelled peas

PREPARATION

▧ *Preheat the oven. Melt the butter over a medium heat on top of the stove.*
▧ *Chop the onion and brown it lightly.*
▧ *Add rice and cook on for a further 3–4 minutes, then pour in the bouillon and add the garlic, bay leaves, and salt to taste.*
▧ *Cover and bake in the oven for about 20 minutes, or until the rice is tender.*
▧ *While the rice is cooking, finely dice the ham, then add the ham and the peas to the cooked rice, mix in lightly with a fork and serve immediately.*

Desserts

Apricot Tart 103

Almond Gateau 104

Apple Fritters 105

Almond Petits Fours 106

Creme Caramel 107

'Burned Cream' Dessert 108

Custard Flan with Apples 109

Chocolate Mousse 110

Ice Cream 111

Lemon Sorbet 112

Apricot Tart

TARTE AUX ABRICOTS

SERVES 8
Cooking time 25–30 minutes
Oven temperature 175° C/ 350° F/Gas 4
INGREDIENTS
450 g/1 lb sweet *or* puff pastry (*see* Pastry Making)
1 kg/2¼ lb fresh or canned apricots – which should be halves if possible
1 cup/160 g/5½ oz icing (confectioner's) sugar
165 ml/9 tbsp apricot jam

PREPARATION

Line a flan ring with the pastry, prick all over and dust lightly with the icing (confectioner's) sugar.

Halve the apricots and pit them, if fresh. Line the pastry case with the fruit, so that each piece slightly overlaps the one before it. Dust the remaining sugar over the fruit and bake the tart.

As the tart is cooking, melt the jam over gentle heat. Using a pastry brush, glaze the tart with the molten jam as soon as it is cooked.

This tart is at its best still warm from the oven. And when it's at its best, it's very good indeed.

Almond Gâteau

GATEAU DE PITHIVIERS

SERVES 6

Cooking time 25–30 minutes

Oven temperature 200° C/
400° F/Gas 6

INGREDIENTS

675 g/1½ lb puff pastry
(*see* Pastry Making)

Good 1 cup/115 g/4½ oz
ground almonds

½ cup/65 g/2½ oz sugar

60 ml/4 tbsp butter

2 eggs

2 egg yolks

30 ml/2 tbsp rum or brandy

⅔ cup/150 ml/¼ pt double
(heavy) cream

PREPARATION

▉ *Cut two 8 in/20 cm circular bases from the rolled puff pastry. One should be ¼ in/.5 cm thick, the other ⅛ in/ 3 mm.*
▉ *Mix the ground almonds with the sugar.*
▉ *Melt the butter and beat it into the almonds with 1 egg, the egg yolks and the rum or brandy. Whisk in the cream.*
▉ *Place the thinner pastry base on a baking sheet.*
▉ *Fill the middle generously with the almond mixture.*
▉ *Beat the remaining egg and lightly brush the edges of the pastry base with the egg wash.*
▉ *Cover the almond mixture with the thicker pastry lid and press down firmly at the edges: make a good seal.*
▉ *Brush the top of the pastry with the remaining egg wash and bake in that hot oven until the pastry top is golden brown.*
▉ *Serve hot if you can.*

Apple Fritters

BEIGNETS AUX POMMES

SERVES 8

Preparation time 1 hour,
excluding batter

Cooking time 3–4 minutes

INGREDIENTS

1¼ cups/300 ml/½ pt coating
batter (*see* Cook's Tips)

675 g/1½ lb cooking (tart)
apples

Good ⅓ cup/75 g/3 oz sugar

30 ml/2 tbsp rum or kirsch

1¼ cups/300 ml/½ pt cooking
oil

PREPARATION

■ *Peel, core and slice the cooking apples, not too thinly.*
■ *Dredge with half the sugar, sprinkle with the rum or kirsch and set aside for an hour or so.*
■ *When you are ready to fry, wipe the apple slices.*
■ *Dip them in the batter and fry at 180° C/350° F for 3–4 minutes or until golden. Serve very hot.*

COOK'S TIPS

Here is the classic recipe
for batter. You'll need:
225 g/½ lb flour
12 ml/bare tbsp yeast –
half the quantity for dried
60 ml/4 tbsp olive oil
Pinch of salt
1¼ cups/300 ml/½ pt
lukewarm water
2 egg whites
Preparation:
■ Warm the flour slightly
in a bowl and make a well
in the middle.
■ Mix the yeast, oil, salt
and water together. (Use
your fingers – the
mixture is ready when it
just coats them.)
■ Add the yeast mixture
to the flour and blend as
quickly as you can.
■ Let stand in a warm
place for 3–4 hours.
■ Just before frying ,
stiffly beat the egg
whites and fold them into
the mixture.

Almond Petits Fours

PETITS FOURS BERRICHONS

Serves a dinner party if you're lucky
Cooking time 8 minutes
Oven temperature 200° C/ 400° F/Gas 6
INGREDIENTS
4 egg whites
100 g/¼ lb ground almonds
100 g/¼ lb vanilla sugar
60 ml/4 tbsp plain (all-purpose) flour

PREPARATION

▪ *Beat the egg whites very stiffly.*
▪ *Mix the almonds, sugar and flour together and gently fold in the egg whites.*
▪ *Pipe the mixture onto a baking sheet in little piles. Bake.*

COOK'S TIP

This is an excellent petit four base, onto which you can pop any number of enticing little delicacies.
Such as: puréed apple and cinnamon with the odd baked almond on top. Melted chocolate. Coffee butter cream. A little brandy butter with a fresh berry. And so on.
This is the end of the book and you should be learning a little boldness by now.

Crème Caramel

CRÈME AU CARAMEL

SERVES 6

Cooking time 35 minutes

Oven temperature 170° C/
325° F/Gas 3

INGREDIENTS

2 cups/450 ml/¾ pt milk

1 vanilla pod

225 g/½ lb sugar

2 eggs

4 egg yolks

PREPARATION

■ *Heat the milk to boiling point and remove from the heat. Add the vanilla pod and allow it to steep.*
■ *As the vanilla is infusing, dissolve half the sugar in 1¼ cups/300 ml/½ pt water. Boil the sugar and water over a high heat, until the mixture begins to brown — that is, caramelize.*
■ *When the mixture is a light brown, remove the pan from the heat — it will go on colouring by itself.*
■ *Mix the remaining sugar with the eggs and the egg yolks and beat well. Trickle in the hot milk.*
■ *Distribute equal quantities of the caramel mixture between 6 ramekins large enough to hold all the milk mixture. Spread the caramel evenly about the bases if you can.*
■ *Pour some of the milk mixture into each of the ramekins.*
■ *Poach the ramekins uncovered in a water bath in the oven for the allotted span (see Salmon Mousse Chaud-Froid for detailed poaching instructions).*
■ *Chill before serving — in the ramekins or turned out onto a plate.*

'Burned Cream' Dessert

CREME BRULEE

SERVES 6

Cooking time 35–40 minutes

Oven temperature 170° C/
325° F/Gas 3

INGREDIENTS

1 ¼ cups/300 ml/½ pt milk

1 vanilla pod

⅔ cup/150 ml/¼ pt double
(heavy) cream

100 g/¼ lb sugar

2 eggs

4 egg yolks

100 g/¼ lb brown sugar

PREPARATION

■ Preheat the oven. Heat the milk to boiling point on top of the stove, then remove from the heat.

■ Add the vanilla pod and whisk in the cream. Allow to stand for 10 minutes.

■ Mix the sugar with the eggs and the egg yolks and beat well.

■ Trickle in the hot milk and cream and stir thoroughly.

■ Pour the mixture into 6 ramekins and poach them uncovered in a water bath in the oven (see *Salmon Mousse Chaud-Froid* for detailed poaching instructions). The water should not boil.

■ Remove the ramekins from the oven when the mixture is set – 30–35 minutes – and set aside to cool.

■ Immediately before serving, sprinkle the brown sugar evenly over the mixture in the ramekins. Glaze under a very hot grill (broiler) until the sugar bubbles and melts. Serve immediately.

Custard Flan with Apples

FLAN AU LAIT A L'ALSACIENNE

SERVES 8
Cooking time 35–40 minutes
Oven temperature 180° C/ 350 °F/Gas 4

INGREDIENTS
30 ml/2 tbsp butter
275 g/10 oz apples
450 g/1 lb sweet pastry (*see* Sweet Pastry)
1¼ cups/300 ml/½ pt milk
4 eggs
½ cup/100 g/3½ oz sugar
1 vanilla pod

PREPARATION

■ *Preheat the oven. Melt the butter over a low heat on top of the stove.*

■ *Slice the apples and stew them gently for about five minutes in the butter until they are soft.*

■ *Line a flan ring with the pastry and layer the apples over the bottom.*

■ *Heat the milk to boiling point.*

■ *Beat the eggs with the sugar and trickle in the hot milk. Add the vanilla pod.*

■ *Pour the egg milk over the apples up to the rim of the pastry and bake until the custard mixture is set.*

Chocolate Mousse

MOUSSE AU CHOCOLAT

SERVES 6

Cooking time 30 minutes

INGREDIENTS

225 g/½ lb plain chocolate

45 ml/3 tbsp milk

Bare ½ cup/50 g/2 oz icing (confectioner's) sugar

4 eggs

PREPARATION

■ *Over a very low heat indeed, or in a double boiler or double saucepan, melt the chocolate with the milk. Add the icing (confectioner's) sugar.*

■ *Separate the yolks from the whites. Stir the yolks into the chocolate mixture and beat the whites until they are very stiff.*

■ *Fold the peaky whites into the chocolate mixture as gently as possible and pour the mixture into a mould, or individual ramekins, and chill.*

■ *Serve when set – about 20 minutes at the minimum.*

COOK'S TIPS

There are various bits and pieces you can add to this basic recipe. Concentrated orange juice or orange zest, Cointreau, cognac, vodka, and so on. Add these special extras to the main chocolate mixture just before you fold in the egg whites.

Ice Cream

LA GLACE

SERVES 6
Cooking time 20 minutes
Setting time about 2 hours
INGREDIENTS
6 egg yolks
⅔ cup/150 g/5 oz sugar
4 cups/900 ml/1½ pt milk

PREPARATION

■ Beat the egg yolks and the sugar together until the mixture becomes quite pale.
■ Heat the milk to boiling point and trickle it into the egg mixture.
■ Return the mixture to the heat, low, and stir continuously. Cook until it coats the back of a spoon. It must not boil.
■ Allow to cool naturally. Stir occasionally, then freeze until ready to serve.

COOK'S TIPS

This is a basic, light ice cream you can enrich or flavour endlessly.
Add whipped cream to the cooled mixture or egg yolks and sugar (in the proportion of 1 egg yolk to 30 ml/2 tbsp sugar) to the pre-cooked mixture. Heavy concentrations of fruit, coffee and nuts can be added to the cold mixture. Vanilla pods, chocolate or caramel go in at the hot milk stage. Watch the sugar content: taste it when cold but unfrozen and bear in mind that the sensation of sweetness diminishes as the temperature falls, so you may need more than you think.

Lemon Sorbet

SORBET AU CITRON

SERVES 6
Cooking time 50 minutes
Setting time 3–4 hours
INGREDIENTS
2½ cups/600 ml/1 pt water
225 g/½ lb white sugar
6 lemons
1 vanilla pod
1 egg white

PREPARATION

■ *Heat the water to boiling point and stir in the sugar. Ensure it is properly melted.*
■ *Finely grate the zest (rind) of two of the lemons and add, with the vanilla pod, to the syrup. Remove the syrup from the heat and allow to stand for 45 minutes.*
■ *Juice all 6 lemons and strain the juice.*
■ *Strain the lemon and vanilla mixture, and add the lemon juice.*
■ *Stiffly beat the egg white and fold it into the mixture.*
■ *Freeze until ready to serve.*

COOK'S TIP

As with ice creams, sorbets can take on any flavour you wish to give them. Simply add your strained and sweetened fruit purée at the lemon juice point.

Basic Techniques – Addendum

Béchamels and Veloutés

INGREDIENTS

90 ml/6 tbsp butter
½ cup/65 g/2½ oz flour
5 cups/1.1 L/2 pt milk (for béchamel)
5 cups/1.1 L/2 pt stock (for velouté)
Salt and pepper to taste

Both these sauces begin with a roux, a mixture of plain (all-purpose) flour and shortening (usually butter) cooked together for a few minutes before the liquid is added. In the case of béchamel, the liquid is milk. In the case of velouté, stock.

Proceed as follows:

PREPARATION

■ *Melt the butter over a low heat and whisk in the flour thoroughly. Cook gently for 2–3 minutes (see Cook's Tips).*
■ *Warm the milk or stock and add it to the roux, one-third at a time. Whisk well after each addition of liquid.*
■ *When all the liquid is added, bring the sauce to the boil, whisking constantly. Season to taste.*

COOK'S TIPS

You may well read, in bulkier tomes than this, that there are roux of various colours: white, blond and brown. This is so. The colours are obtained by cooking the roux until the flour begins to brown – a question of minutes only. What you do, of course, is cook the roux to suit the stock: white for chicken or fish, blond for veal and brown for beef and game. Béchamels are *always* white, unless you're unlucky enough to find brown milk.

And now to that universal horror, lumps. No problem. Unless truly fist-sized, they will almost certainly cook themselves out, either in the pan or in the dish for which your sauce is eventually intended. But if they remain recalcitrant, strain the sauce or liquidize it.

VARIATIONS

Béchamel and velouté are really building-block sauces to which other ingredients are added. Here are a few famous ones to whet your appetite and imagination.

Béchamel
(for each 2½ cups/600 ml/1 pt)

MORNAY
60 ml/4 tbsp grated Parmesan
60 ml/4 tbsp double or single (heavy or light) cream

NANTUA
60 ml/4 tbsp crayfish butter
4 crayfish tails

SOUBISE
225 g/½ lb sliced onions, cooked until soft in butter
⅔ cup/150 ml/¼ pt double or single (heavy or light) cream

ITALIAN-STYLE, FOR USE WITH OVEN-BAKED PASTA:
60 ml/4 tbsp grated Parmesan
large pinch grated nutmeg

Velouté
(for each 2½ cups/600 ml/1 pt)

ANCHOIS
4 chopped anchovy fillets

AURORE
⅔ cup/150 ml/¼ pt tomato sauce
60 ml/4 tbsp butter

BERCY
½ cup/50 g/2 oz chopped shallots
⅔ cup/150 ml/¼ pt dry white wine
15 ml/1 tbsp chopped parsley

RAVIGOTE
⅔ cup/150 ml/¼ pt dry white wine
60 ml/4 tbsp white wine vinegar
30 ml/2 tbsp chopped tarragon, chives and chervil

And so on. Needless to say, cook the sauce on until the various nuances blend and, if you've added extra liquid, reduce by boiling or simmering it back to its original volume. But do it carefully, for flour-thickened sauces can easily burn.
For a complete change of taste use scallop liquor, vermouth, mustard and cayenne pepper – see the recipe for Gratinée of Scallops.

Court Bouillons and Poaching Liquids

INGREDIENTS

5 Am pt/2.25 L/4 pt water
225 g/½ lb sliced carrots
225 g/½ lb sliced onions
1 sprig fresh thyme
2 bay leaves
30 ml/2 tbsp fresh chopped parsley
⅔ cup/150 ml/¼ pt white wine vinegar or lemon juice
12 peppercorns

To begin with, a court bouillon is not a stock, although if strained and re-used often enough – a perfectly permissible procedure – it may turn into one. The confusion arises from the frequent use of the word 'bouillon' as a synonym for 'stock'. A court bouillon on the other hand is simply a liquor for poaching fish. Here is a typical recipe:

PREPARATION

■ *Bring all the ingredients to the boil bar the peppercorns. Simmer for 30 minutes, then add the peppercorns.*
■ *Simmer for a further 10 minutes. Strain and continue with the respective recipe.*

COOK'S ASIDE

This recipe should give you the general idea. Permissible variations include the addition of milk – for such fish as turbot or brill – or dry white wine. Lobster and crab need only plain, salted – some say sea-water.
Other points to watch are:
■ Start large fish in cold court bouillon. Indeed, it is often sufficient to bring such a beast to the boil and then let it cool again, when it will be cooked, as the menus say, to perfection.
■ Strain your court bouillon if you wish to re-use it. It can also be frozen.

Aspics and Chaud-Froids

INGREDIENTS

10 sheets of leaf gelatin(e)
or
30 ml/2 tbsp granular gelatin(e)
90 ml/6 tbsp hot water
2½ cups/600 ml/1 pt clear stock (for an aspic jelly)
or
2½ cups/600 ml/1 pt velouté or béchamel (for a chaud-froid)
Seasoning (*see* Cook's tip)

When and if you make your glazes (see Stocks and Glazes) you will discover that they set into firm jellies very much of their own accord. Indeed, even lightly reduced stocks will sometimes set: it all depends on the gelatinous content of the bones. In due course, this will bring us round to gelatin(e). But let us first remark that true aspic jellies – and chaud-froids, their velouté- or béchamel-based partners (see Béchamels and Veloutés) – should really be set with the stock or glaze of the item for which they are intended.

In practice, however, even the best professional kitchens make liberal use of gelatin(e). And this is how they do it.

PREPARATION

■ *Melt the gelatin(e) in the hot water.*
■ *Heat, but do not boil, the stock, velouté or béchamel. Whisk in the water and gelatin(e) – ensure it is well distributed.*
■ *Allow the mixture to cool to lukewarm. It is now ready for use (see Salmon Mousse Chaud-Froid and Chicken Livers in Aspic).*

COOK'S TIPS

You may flavour or tint these sauces to your heart's content. Tarragon is a common choice for aspic and turmeric (yellow) or puréed spinach, squeezed dry (green), for the chaud-froids.

Pastry Making

INGREDIENTS

225 g/½ lb plain (all-purpose) flour
1 pinch salt
½ cup/100 g/¼ lb butter
About ¾ cup/200 ml/7 fl oz water

Despite what is written in the Sunday papers, professional kitchens are not quiet and contemplative salons where fine-minded artists congregate to discuss their works in subdued and mellifluous murmurs. From the highest to the lowest, a great deal of swearing, shouting and outright argument goes on, many short cuts are taken and food, from scalding hot to freezing, is more often dealt with by hand than by instrument. The hand, in fact, is the kitchen's most useful tool.

This professional impatience has a direct bearing on pastry. Puff is invariably bought in, frozen. The product is uniformly good and we advise you to patronize it.

Short-crust, on the other hand, is easy, cheap and, most important of all, takes only seconds to make.

PREPARATION

▌*Sieve the flour and salt together. Rub in the butter until the mixture takes the form of fine crumbs.*
▌*Add the water slowly until the pastry has a good, firm rolling consistency. (Do not over-handle. Use fingers: they are cooler than hands.)*
▌*If you have the time, let the pastry stand – wrapped to keep in the moisture – for a couple of hours in a cool place.*

SWEET PASTRY
▌*Add 15 g/½ oz of sugar at the butter stage.*

Stocks and Glazes

INGREDIENTS
PER 2½ CUPS/600 ML/1 PT WATER ADD
450 g/1 lb bones – fish or meat
1 onion, sliced
1 carrot, sliced
1 small fennel bulb, sliced (optional)
1 celery stalk, sliced
Any meat or fish trimmings except fat or suet
No seasoning

It is still rare to find proper stocks and glazes in domestic kitchens. Why? In the bygone times when I had a day job, and simply cooked at night for friends, I would regularly arrive home at around 6.30 with bags of raw food for a dinner I wanted to eat at nine.

First things? Grab the two biggest pans, onions, carrots, bay and fish bones into one, ditto and meat bones into the other. Get the stocks on. Then carry on with the rest. The fish stock takes about 40 minutes. Strain carefully, then keep on reducing. The meat I left until the last moment.

In any event, a preparation time of 2 to 3 hours is actually ample time to make stock and then turn your stock into that viscous, honest version of the stock (bouillon) cube – the glaze – which is simply a very heavily reduced stock. And if you're still uncertain, read on.

PREPARATION

■ Bring the ingredients to the boil in the right amount of water.
■ Lower the heat to a gentle simmer.
■ If you are making a fish stock, remove from the heat and strain carefully after 40 minutes.
■ Cook meat stocks for up to 8 hours, then strain carefully.

COOK'S TIP

Note that no seasoning is recommended for stocks. This is to give your cooking flexibility. For if you do season, and then go on to reduce your strained stock to the sauce-like consistency of a glaze, you will be seriously stuck with the equally concentrated and uncompromising taste of the seasoning. Season last, when the texture and thickness are as you wish them. Incidentally, to turn a stock into a glaze usually requires a reduction of at least 75 per cent.
For the rest, your stock, as it cooks, will look after itself provided that you:
■ Skim it occasionally, lifting off scum or fat with a broad flat spoon.
■ Do not boil it until it has been skimmed and strained, or you risk emulsifying the fats and giving your stock a cloudy consistency and muddy taste.
■ Expect nothing too sophisticated from pork or lamb bones. In professional kitchens, such meats should not be used for stocks unless as a basis for hearty, thickened soups.
But if lamb or pork is all you have, don't be deterred. Just skim more frequently.
■ The permanently boiling restaurant stockpot is a fiction, by the way. It will not have been in the same place for 20 years. Rather, some underpaid commis will have begun it in the early morning, fresh for the day.
■ If you have oodles of time, fat can be removed from a stock by chilling it. The fat then solidifies and can be removed from the top of the jellied stock.

Hollandaise

Cooking time 5–10 minutes

INGREDIENTS

4 egg yolks

15 ml/1 tbsp cold water

5 ml/1 tsp lemon juice

225 g/½ lb butter

If you fancy yourself as a chef and you cannot make these two sauces, stop. Do not boil another egg until you have taken this book into your kitchen and taught yourself how. Buy yourself a piece of fish to eat with the Hollandaise if you need an incentive: the mayonnaise will keep until Sunday.

PREPARATION

▇ *Put the yolks, water and lemon juice into the thickest pan you have. Set the pan in a bain-marie or water bath at low heat. Whisk the mixture until it thickens a little.*
▇ *In the meantime, gently melt the butter. It should remain lukewarm.*
▇ *Whisking all the while, add the butter to the eggs, one-third at a time. Whisk the mixture until it thickens again before adding more.*
▇ *Cook gently on until you have the consistency of thick cream. Hollandaise is always served luke warm.*

CHEF'S ASIDES

All this sauce needs is a gentle touch: gentle heat, the gradual addition of the butter and no more than 90 ml/5 tbsp of butter per yolk.
If the egg and butter separate – ie the emulsion is lost – whisk in a couple of tablespoons of boiling water. But make sure you have not exceeded the crucial egg/butter relationship.
If you overcook the egg and it begins to granulate – or scramble, as we call it at breakfast time – whisk in a couple of ice cubes. This thickens the butter and disguises your blunder somewhat.

Mayonnaise

SERVES 6–7

INGREDIENTS

3–4 egg yolks

15 ml/1 tbsp vinegar

5 ml/1 tsp English mustard (optional)

2½ cups/600 ml/1 pt olive – or other good – oil

PREPARATION

▇ *Whisk together the eggs, half the vinegar and the mustard, if you're using it. (Use a blender if you wish.)*
▇ *Add the oil in a very thin stream, whisking constantly. As the mixture thickens and the oil 'disappears' into the eggs, you may increase the flow.*
▇ *Beat until the mixture has emulsified into a creamy dressing. Add the remaining vinegar and season.*

COOK'S TIPS

Since emulsification is facilitated by warmth, make sure the eggs and oil are at room temperature or slightly above. Not straight from the refrigerator in other words.
If the mixture splits, treat it as oil and beat it slowly back into another egg yolk.

VARIATIONS

Both these sauces are regularly used as a basis for further experiment. Here are one or two examples:

With Hollandaise
BÉARNAISE
Either cheat and add tarragon at the end or reduce ⅔ cup/150 ml/¼ pt vinegar and 1 tbsp/15 ml of chopped tarragon to almost nothing before you start with the eggs. Omit the lemon juice.
CHORON
Tint the finished Hollandaise pink with tomato purée (paste).
MOUSSELINE
Fold into the Hollandaise half its volume of whipped cream.

With Mayonnaise
AIÖLI
Heavily load your mayonnaise with fresh crushed garlic.
ROUILLE
(*See* Provençal Fish Soup and Marseilles Fish Stew [Bouillabaisse]) tint the mayonnaise rust-red with paprika, load with garlic and season to taste with cayenne pepper. It should be distinctly tangy.
SAUCE VERTE
A mayonnaise flavoured and coloured with puréed spinach and/or watercress squeezed very dry.

Vinaigrette

The fact that this dressing bears such a name does not mean it should taste of vinegar. At the very most, use ⅓ vinegar (or other acid – lemon juice, for example) to ⅔ oil. The Italians often dispense with the vinegar altogether.

What can be added to a vinaigrette?

▌ Prepared mustard. But take care. Proprietary mustards contain vinegar.

▌ Herbs, fresh or dried, and garlic, of course.

▌ Salt and pepper.

But the best ingredients remain the best oil and, it must be said, the best vinegar your purse will tolerate.

Thickening Methods

The best thickening method I know is a constant diet of foie gras *and chocolate mousse but this is neither the time nor the place for facetious remarks. Let us be serious, then, as serious as the family mausoleum on a grim January dawn. You have before you a sauce, or a casserole, or a gravy thin enough to pass for richly coloured water. What do you do? If you have a gravy nothing. Gravies are not supposed to be thickened. They are best left as an amalgam of pan juices and wine, with a little stock perhaps, although you can boil them down slightly if you wish. Which brings us to:*

REDUCTION

The cleanest way of thickening a sauce or casserole is simply to reduce its water content by boiling, a method with the added advantage of intensifying the taste of the item in question. Just make sure that the seasoning is not too intense to start with. And if you plan to thicken a casserole this way and its principal ingredients are already properly cooked, strain out and reserve them before you reduce the cooking liquid.

BEURRE MANIÉ

Knead together a good ½ cup/75 g/3 oz of flour and 90 ml/5 tbsp of butter into a well-mixed dough. Break the dough – beurre manié – into small chunks and stir it into the hot liquid. The quantity here will very appreciably thicken 5–6¼ cups/1.1–1.4 L/2–2½ pints of liquid. When your sauce is as thick as you want it, keep it on the heat for at least five minutes to cook out any flouriness.

CREAM

Double (heavy) cream added to a sauce you wish to reduce will considerably diminish the reduction time.

EGGS AND BUTTER

Egg yolks whisked into a sauce below boiling point will thicken the sauce as the eggs themselves begin to cook. Three yolks per pint will have their effect, although the sauce itself should always be cream, velouté or béchamel-based.

For extra lustre and some slight thickening, you may also whisk in cold butter. But once again, the sauce must be below boiling point.

Since eggs and butter work, it follows that so will Hollandaise, which is often whisked into cream and fish stock sauces or into fish veloutés just before serving.

Boning and Other Knifework

In this highly truncated butchery section, we look at three techniques for fish and the jointing and boning of fowl. Perhaps boning seems to you too arcane and difficult a task.

It should not. Firstly, it is easy. And secondly, the results are miraculous. Not only is carving made stupefyingly simple but portions soar. Boned and sliced, a good-sized chicken will feed six and two pheasants six to seven. A boon and no mistake. But first the fish.

LARGE FLATFISH INTO STEAKS (OR DARNES)
▓ *Clean the fish, then lay it on a board, either side up.*
▓ *Cut cleanly through the head and along the backbone to the tail.*
▓ *With scissors, snip off the fins from the back and belly.*
▓ *Cut away the head parts.*
▓ *At right angles to your original cut, slice the fish into darnes as thick as you require them.*

SMALL FLATFISH INTO FILLETS
On each side in turn:
▓ *Make a long cut along the backbone.*
▓ *Slide the blade of the knife into the cut at the base of the head.*
▓ *In long and sweeping strokes, run it along the ribs beneath the fillet until the flesh is held by the skin only at belly or back.*
▓ *Cut each fillet away with knife or scissors.*
▓ *To skin, cut through the flesh to the skin at the thinnest end. Holding the fillet firmly, slide the knife between flesh and skin, slowly peeling back the skin.*

LARGE SALMON-SHAPED FISH
Clean these fish either by:
▓ *Slitting the belly from gills to tail or*
▓ *Remove the head and gills and pull out the guts with the hooked end of a ladle or similar.*
De-scale by:
▓ *Grasping the fish firmly by the tail, and with your knife at right angles to the skin, scrape the fish vigorously against the grain of the scale. (Do this underwater if your sink is big enough. Otherwise scales fly.)*

Boning Chicken or other Fowl

This is easy. Just give yourself plenty of time. Your first attempt will take about half an hour. Practice will get you down to five minutes, desperation even less. And re- member, your boned chicken takes less time to cook and therefore stays more moist.

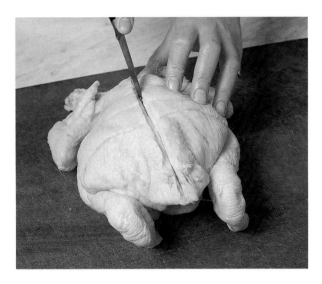

1 Lay the chicken breast side down and make one long cut along the backbone.

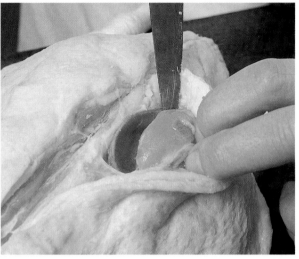

2 Locate the 'oysters', two little pockets of flesh imme- diately in front of the leg joints. Cut them away from the backbone. Dislocate the legs and cut through the joints. Holding the knife flat to the bone, lift the skin away from each side of the pelvic girdle. Pull the legs away from the backbone.

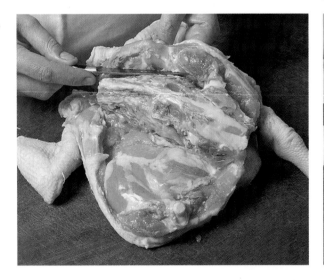

3 Now continue up each side of the backbone, scraping the flesh away from the rib-cage. When you encounter the shoulder blades, cut the skin covering away by sliding the knife beneath it, but do not cut the skin. Once the skin is well clear of the shoulder blades, run your fingers down each one to the wing joint. Move the wing with the other hand to help you find it. One short, sharp cut down will sever the joint. Sever both and continue working down the rib cage until the ribs stand proud.

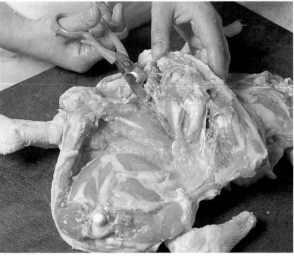

4 Cut away the rib cage with scissors, leaving the breast bone still attached.

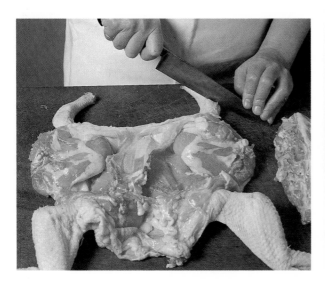

5 Now for the legs. Cut round the leg knuckles to sever the tendons.

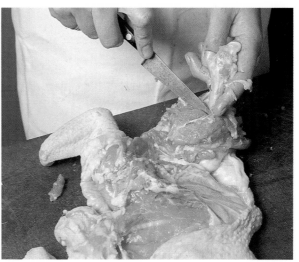

6 Push the leg meat down to the next knuckle with the knife blade against the bone to free the thigh bone. Repeat with the other leg.

7 Repeat the process to the feet of both legs, then cut the feet away.

8 Cut the pinions away from the wings.

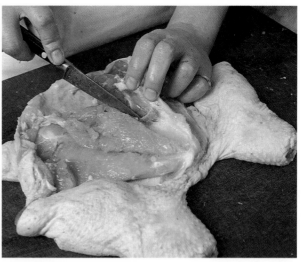

9 Push the wing meat down as you did for the leg bones.

10 Free the breastbone, gently working from the middle to the tail.

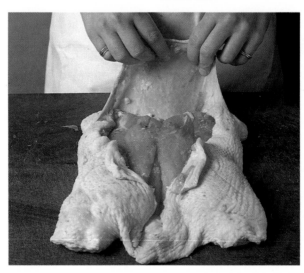

11 Your chicken is now boned. Blanket-stitch it up with a skewer or two along the original vertebral cut and fire away.

JOINTING A CHICKEN

■ With the bird on its back, cut through the loose skin around the leg joints. Dislocate each leg and cut through the joint. Remove the feet.

■ Now cut the bird in two halves lengthways, separating the breasts from the backbone.

■ Trim the backbone of loose scraps and cut in two parts, slicing it at right angles to the backbone.

■ Take the breasts and wings and place them on the board with the breasts uppermost.

■ With the blade close to the high ridge of the breast-bone, run the knife along the breast, blade straight down, until you meet the wishbone. Break it and continue the cut.

■ The breast will now fall away from the breastbone. Remove it and the whole wing. Look at it carefully. You will find a thin, crescent-shaped sliver of meat scarcely attached to the breast meat. Pull it away and set it aside (see *Warm Salad of Duck and Chicken Mignons*). Remove the other breast – or *suprême* – in the same way.

■ Cut away the last joint of each wing, leaving half a wing attached to each breast.

■ Finally, cut away the skin and meat from the wing bone still attached to give your chicken *suprêmes* an attractive bone handle.

Conclusion

A lot of serious nonsense is talked about art and cooking. Chefs these days, according to many a tubby little journalist too greedy to know better, are latter-day Michelangelos whose raison-d'être is not hospitality but aesthetic experimenting. This is, of course, another journalistic invention like nouvelle cuisine, the guiding principles of which have been well known to French cooks for a not-so-nouvelle two hundred years.

Unfortunately, many chefs have now taken to reading smart newspapers and are beginning to believe what they read. This generally means that prices go up. For naturally, when a salmon quenelle has been elevated to the status of a work of art, we must also pay for the pleasure of its company, as well as for the raw materials and skill that went into making it.

But this art business has a worse effect yet. It mystifies. Your dish is not simply a collection of ingredients and a recipe, it is something more, something finer, more intangible, something . . . yes, beyond the reach of ordinary clods. In truth, what is set enticingly before you is nothing other than ingredients and a recipe. And at one point in his life, the chap who cooked it for you could not have boiled an egg.

Index

NOTE: Where a second, alternative recipe title is given in French, it is printed in italics in the index.